U.S. Fish & Wildlife Service

Izembek
National Wildlife Refuge
Land Exchange/Road Corridor

Draft Environmental Impact Statement

Executive Summary

U.S. Fish & Wildlife Service

TABLE OF CONTENTS

LIST OF TABLES

LIST OF FIGURES

LIST OF ACRONYMS

2003 EIS	King Cove Access Project Environmental Impact Statement (USACE 2003)
Act	Omnibus Public Land Management Act of 2009; Public Law 111-11, Title VI, Subtitle E
ANCSA	Alaska Native Claims Settlement Act
ANILCA	Alaska National Interest Lands Conservation Act
Coast Guard	U.S. Coast Guard
Corps	U.S. Army Corps of Engineers
EIS	Environmental Impact Statement
NEPA	National Environmental Policy Act
Selected Lands	King Cove Corporation lands selected under rights under the *Alaska Native Claims Settlement Act* (ANCSA)
Service	U.S. Fish and & Wildlife Service
U.S.	United States of America
USC	United States Code

LIST OF REFERENCES

FAA (Federal Aviation Administration). 2010. U.S. Terminal Procedures Publication. Alaska Volume 1 of 1. Effective 23 September 2010 to 18 November 2010.

USACE (U.S. Army Corps of Engineers). 2003. King Cove Access Project Environmental Impact Statement. Alaska District, Anchorage, Alaska. Draft July 2003. Final December 2003. Record of Decision January 22, 2004.

Walker, A. M. 2010. Personal communication regarding operations of the King Cove Airport. Aviation Safety and Security Officer. Central Region, Alaska Department of Transportation and Public Facilities. November 1, 2010. Joan Kluwe. URS.

ES-1 EXECUTIVE SUMMARY

ES-1.1   Introduction

In the *Omnibus Public Land Management Act of 2009* (Public Law 111-11, Title VI, Subtitle E) (Act), Congress authorized the Secretary of the Interior to exchange lands within the Izembek National Wildlife Refuge for lands owned by the State of Alaska and the King Cove Corporation for the purpose of constructing a single lane gravel road between the communities of King Cove and Cold Bay, Alaska if it is in the public interest. In the Act, Congress directed the Secretary of the Interior to prepare an Environmental Impact Statement (EIS) in accordance with the terms of the Act and the *National Environmental Policy Act of 1969* (NEPA), as amended (42 USC 4321 et. seq.), and its implementing regulations (40 CFR Parts 1500-1508). Congress specified that the EIS must analyze the land exchange, potential road construction and operation, and a specific road corridor through the Izembek National Wildlife Refuge and the Izembek Wilderness that is to be identified in consultation with the State of Alaska, the City of King Cove, and the Agdaagux Tribe of King Cove (Section 6402(b)(2)). Upon completion of the EIS, the Act requires the Secretary of Interior to determine whether the proposed land exchange and road is in the public interest.

If determined to be in the public interest, the land exchange would enable construction and operation of a single lane gravel road between the communities of King Cove and Cold Bay, Alaska, that would provide King Cove residents road access to the Cold Bay Airport. Congress responded to continuing concerns about reliable access for health and safety purposes on the part of the King Cove Corporation, the City of King Cove, the Aleutians East Borough, and the Agdaagux Tribe of King Cove.

The U.S. Fish and Wildlife Service (Service) is the lead federal agency for the EIS. Cooperating agencies are:

Federal:	U.S. Army Corps of Engineers, Alaska District (Corps) Federal Highway Administration/Western Federal Lands
Tribal:	Agdaagux Tribe of King Cove Native Village of Belkofski
State:	State of Alaska
Borough:	Aleutians East Borough
Local/Other:	City of King Cove King Cove Corporation

ES-1.2   Proposed Action

The proposed action is the exchange of land between the federal government, the State of Alaska, and the King Cove Corporation for the purpose of constructing and operating a single lane gravel road between the communities of King Cove and Cold Bay, Alaska. As provided in the Act, the road "shall be used primarily for health and safety purposes, (including access to and from the Cold Bay Airport) and only for noncommercial purposes." The use of taxis, commercial vans for public transportation, and shared rides is exempted from the prohibition on commercial uses of the road.

Congress identified the federal and non-federal lands involved in the exchange and provided guidance regarding the administration of the exchanged lands (Sections 6401 and 6404 of the Act) (Figure ES-1). Legal descriptions of lands proposed for exchange are included in Appendix B of the Draft EIS.

- Approximately 206 acres of federal land (surface and subsurface estate) of the Izembek National Wildlife Refuge would be conveyed to the State under the land exchange. The final acreage to be exchanged would be determined by the width and location of the road corridor including safety turnouts as determined in each of the road alternatives considered. The boundary of the Izembek Wilderness would be modified to exclude the road corridor. (The specific lands to be exchanged for the road corridor were not identified in the Act; 2 road corridor alternatives are evaluated in this EIS.)

- Approximately 1,600 acres (surface and subsurface estate) within the Alaska Maritime National Wildlife Refuge on Sitkinak Island, including land withdrawn for use by the U.S. Coast Guard (Coast Guard) and approximately 170 acres of refuge-managed land would be transferred to the State.

- Approximately 43,093 acres of land owned by the State of Alaska, adjacent to the North Creek and Pavlof Units of the Alaska Peninsula National Wildlife Refuge, would be conveyed to the United States (U.S.) and added to the Alaska Peninsula National Wildlife Refuge as wilderness. This includes the subsurface estate, but does not include submerged lands including tidelands, lakes, rivers, and streams to be retained by the State of Alaska.

- Approximately 13,300 acres of land owned by King Cove Corporation (surface estate but excluding tidelands and submerged land of rivers, streams, and lakes determined navigable for purposes of title through federal judicial or administrative procedures), located near Mortensens Lagoon and the mouth of Kinzarof Lagoon, would be conveyed to the U.S. and added to the Izembek National Wildlife Refuge. The Kinzarof Lagoon parcel would also be added to Izembek Wilderness. As a part of the exchange, the King Cove Corporation would also relinquish its selection of 5,430 acres in Izembek Wilderness (selected lands) on the east side of Cold Bay made under the terms of the *Alaska Native Claims Settlement Act* (ANCSA).

The Act directed that the exchange could not be finalized before the parcel of state land located in Kinzarof Lagoon had been designated as part of the State of Alaska Izembek State Game Refuge. The Alaska Legislature passed and the Governor signed the *Izembek State Game Refuge Land Exchange Bill* into law (HB 210 Chapter 119 SLA 10) satisfying this requirement.

The proposed road corridor would connect the road terminus at the Northeast Hovercraft Terminal, approved in the King Cove Access Project EIS (2003 EIS) (USACE 2003), which is approximately 22 miles north of the City of King Cove, with the existing Cold Bay road system. Two road corridor alternatives are evaluated in this EIS. Both were developed in consultation with the State, the City of King Cove, and the Agdaagux Tribe of King Cove as required by Section 6402 (b)(2) of the Act.

Figure ES-1 Project Area Map

Map Symbols

- Proposed Route
- Wilderness Trails
- Existing Roads and Trails
- Under Construction
- Izembek National Wildlife Refuge
- Designated Wilderness
- Alaska Peninsula National Wildlife Refuge
- Other National Wildlife Refuge Areas
- State
- Other Federal
- King Cove Corporation Conveyed
- Other Private

Proposed Exchange Land

- Lands to go to the Service
- Selected Lands to be Relinquished*
- Service Lands to go to State of Alaska

*Other Alaska Native Corporation selected lands exist within the region, however, only the King Cove Corporation selected land parcel proposed for exchange is displayed on this map.

Approximately 43,093 acres of state land proposed to transfer to the U.S.

Approximately 206 acres of federal land (road corridor) proposed for transfer to the State. The corridor for transfer would accomodate only one of the two proposed road alignments.

Approximately 13,300 acres of land owned by King Cove Corporation proposed for transfer to the U.S. including approximately 5,430 acres, for which King Cove Corporation would relinquish selection.

Approximately 1,600 acres of federal land proposed for transfer to the State.

SITKINAK ISLAND

IZEMBEK NATIONAL WILDLIFE REFUGE
LAND EXCHANGE/ROAD CORRIDOR EIS

PROJECT AREA
MAP

ALASKA PENINSULA, ALASKA

URS

The proposed road corridor would be approximately 19.4 to 21.6 miles long and 100 feet wide. The proposed routes would cross Izembek National Wildlife Refuge (including Izembek Wilderness) and lands owned by the King Cove Corporation. The Service would execute an administrative boundary adjustment in the vicinity of Blinn Lake; an area that is currently designated as Alaska Peninsula National Wildlife Refuge, but administered by Izembek National Wildlife Refuge, would become part of Izembek National Wildlife Refuge. As directed in Section 6402 (f), both of the proposed road corridors evaluated in this EIS were designed to minimize adverse impacts to refuge resources, require the transfer of the minimum acreage of federal land, and to the maximum extent practicable, incorporate existing roads into the corridor.

The proposed road would be single lane (i.e., 13 feet wide), gravel surfaced with appropriate safety turnouts (11 feet wide), and a chain barrier or bollard barrier on each side. The average road footprint width would be 41.4 to 47.6 feet for the central and southern alignments, respectively. These features meet design requirements established by the Act in Section 6043(a). If the Secretary of the Interior finds that a land exchange is in the public interest, an enforceable mitigation plan for road design and construction as required in Section 6043(e) will be developed as a part of the land exchange process, building upon mitigation measures identified as part of this EIS, with provisions to avoid wildlife and fish impacts and to mitigate wetlands loss.

Should the land exchange be found in the public interest but a construction permit is not authorized, or upon expiration of congressional legislative authority, the land exchange would be void, and federal and non-federal lands would remain in, or would be returned to, the ownership status prior to the exchange (Section 6406 of the Act). In general, the Act's legislative authority expires 7 years from the date of the Act, unless a construction permit has been issued. Upon issuance of a construction permit, legislative authority would be extended for 5 additional years.

ES-1.3   Purpose and Need

The purpose of the proposed land exchange, as provided in the Act, is to transfer to the State of Alaska all right, title, and interest to a road corridor that would allow the construction, operation, and maintenance of a single lane gravel road between the communities of King Cove and Cold Bay, Alaska. The proposed road is to be used primarily to address health and safety issues, including reliable access to and from the Cold Bay Airport, and only for noncommercial purposes.

If the Secretary of the Interior finds that a land exchange and construction of the proposed road is in the public interest, then the applicant (not currently defined, but likely to be the State of Alaska) would submit an application to the Corps which would then determine compliance with the *Clean Water Act* Section 404 (b) (1) Guidelines.

In carrying out its compliance responsibilities, the Corps must define the basic and overall project purpose. The basic purpose is used to determine if a given project is water dependent and requires access or proximity to, or siting within, a special aquatic site to fulfill its basic purpose. The overall purpose is an independent assessment of the project purpose by the Corps to accommodate a range of alternatives for consideration and to determine the least environmentally damaging practicable alternative. The basic project purpose is to provide a transportation system between the City of King Cove and the Cold Bay Airport. The overall project purpose is to construct a long term, safe, and reliable year round transportation system between the cities of King Cove and Cold Bay.

Objectives to be achieved by the proposed action include:

- Providing a safe, reliable, affordable transportation system between the City of King Cove and the airport in Cold Bay, Alaska;

- Addressing health and safety issues for King Cove residents, including timely emergency medical evacuations when needed and improved access to health care services not available in King Cove through access to the Cold Bay Airport;

- Balancing the needs of the communities, the national wildlife refuges (including wilderness), and ecosystem functions in the area;

- Transferring the minimum federal acreage necessary for the proposed road corridor;

- Developing an environmentally sensitive project design to minimize impact to wildlife, fish, plants, and their habitats, subsistence uses, wilderness character, and wetlands; and

- Selecting a road corridor that makes use of existing trails and roads to the maximum extent practicable.

The need for the proposed action is broader than the focused purpose specified in the Act. The project needs arise from the underlying issues related to transportation to and from the community of King Cove. Three needs are identified: health and safety, quality of life, and affordable transportation.

Health and Safety: Reliable and Safe Transportation for Medical Care, including Emergencies and Evacuations

The State of Alaska, City of King Cove, King Cove Corporation, Agdaagux Tribe of King Cove, and Aleutians East Borough have identified the need for a road connecting the City of King Cove to the Cold Bay Airport as the only safe, reliable, and affordable means for year round access to medical services not available in King Cove, including infrequent, but time-sensitive medical emergency evacuations. Residents of the City of King Cove believe a road is necessary due to the limitations of medical care available in the region.

For cases requiring emergency care exceeding that available at the King Cove Clinic, medical evacuations from the King Cove community arrive first at the Cold Bay Airport via aircraft, hovercraft, and marine vessels, depending upon weather conditions and availability of transport modes. Helicopters are not always available, as they must be mobilized from as far away as St. Paul Island, where Coast Guard Search and Rescue helicopters are stationed. During the winter commercial fishing season, Coast Guard helicopters are temporarily stationed at Cold Bay to monitor commercial fishing and to provide emergency medical evacuations from commercial fishing vessels in the Bering Sea and Pacific Ocean. At the airport, assistance is provided by the Anna Livingston Memorial Clinic. The clinic does not have full time physicians on staff and has less medical staff available than the King Cove Clinic. Evacuated patients are then transported to medical facilities offering more advanced care in Anchorage, Alaska, Seattle, Washington, or elsewhere. Other options for emergency medical evacuation services are not available.

The Cold Bay Airport has one of the longest civilian paved runways in Alaska at 10,415 feet and has the only crosswind runway in the vicinity of King Cove and Cold Bay. It has fully operational instrument approach capabilities. The King Cove Airport has a 3,500-foot gravel runway equipped with medium intensity runway lighting, runway end identifier lights, and an automated surface weather observation system. The runway has a non-precision instrument approach procedure, which is limited to approaching only from the east. By federal regulations, the instrument approach procedure for King Cove Airport is not authorized at night and the final 5.2 mile leg should be flown visually (FAA 2010). The State of Alaska recommends daytime-only use of the runway due to topographic obstructions on the approaches and unpredictable winds (Walker 2010).

A hovercraft began operating in 2007 when service was established as a result of the 2003 EIS and Record of Decision (USACE 2003). The hovercraft service was established to improve access to the Cold Bay Airport for health and safety needs, and other general transportation purposes. The hovercraft was operated by the Aleutians East Borough, but operations did not attain the frequency of service proposed in the 2003 EIS nor the projected revenues. Higher than anticipated costs, including the costs of retaining sufficient available trained captains and crew, a low operational threshold for freezing temperatures (icing), wind speed, and wave height were factors in the suspension of hovercraft service in November 2010. To date, operations have not resumed. Upon completion of the permitted road and Northeast Hovercraft Terminal, the Aleutians East Borough may attempt to reinstitute hovercraft service between the new Northeast Hovercraft Terminal and Cross Wind Cove Terminal. The estimated completion date of the permitted road and terminal facility is in the latter part of 2012.

As the Draft EIS was approaching completion, the Aleutians East Borough sent the Service a letter stating they will not resume hovercraft service in the foreseeable future. Due to the timing of the letter, we are unable to restructure the analysis of consequences to reflect this change in the Draft EIS. The Final EIS will reflect this change and other changes that are made in response to public comments.

When weather and other factors restrict use of aircraft or the hovercraft, private fishing vessels have been used to transport passengers, including medical emergencies, to the Cold Bay Dock. Severe weather can prevent safe operations or access by fishing vessels because the community of Cold Bay does not have a boat harbor. Boat access is limited to the Cold Bay Dock, where passengers either have to climb a steel ladder, or are lifted to the deck of the dock via a winch system used to load/unload cargo from fishing boats.

Residents of the City of King Cove emphasize that access to the Cold Bay Airport is essential. Safe and reliable transportation to advanced medical care, including emergency medical care, is not available. They state that the proposed land exchange and construction of a road to the airport in Cold Bay will establish a safe and reliable land connection between the communities and provide access to advanced and emergency medical care.

Quality of Life

Residents of the City of King Cove state that improved access to the Cold Bay Airport would enhance their quality of life by providing reliable access the Cold Bay Airport, and from there to Anchorage and Seattle for health care services, including emergency medical evacuations when needed. King Cove residents have stated that a road would eliminate most of the issues about the unreliability of the current transportation modes in accessing the Cold Bay Airport. Road access would provide peace of mind, particularly during extended periods of inclement weather that prevent marine and air travel. In addition, access to the Cold Bay Airport would provide the students, school board, borough assembly members, and medical service providers residing in King Cove with enhanced opportunities to travel out of their community. Residents would be able to meet with government officials in Anchorage and Juneau more reliably and to visit extended families living in other communities.

Affordable Transportation

Affordable, reliable, and practical transportation is not available for the residents of the City of King Cove to access the Cold Bay Airport. Air transportation is limited by weather, availability of aircraft, and the topographic constraints of the King Cove Airport. Similar to other rural communities in Alaska, flights to and from the King Cove Airport are sometimes delayed or cancelled due to weather. Cost can be an issue for King Cove residents, not all of whom can afford air fares for a family flying back and forth between the communities of King Cove and Cold Bay, or the associated lodging costs when a continuing flight out of Cold Bay is missed or when weather prevents getting back to King Cove from Cold Bay on a return trip.

The hovercraft service has proven more expensive and more difficult to keep in service than originally expected. Ridership and associated revenues have been lower and operations and maintenance costs higher than projected. Keeping the minimum number of trained crew required for operations, including backup when crewmembers are sick, has been difficult and has resulted in cancellation of scheduled service. Operating thresholds include wave heights not exceeding 6 feet and wind speeds not exceeding 30 miles per hour. In addition, freezing temperatures cause operational challenges (icing), which sometimes inhibit hovercraft service.

The State of Alaska, City of King Cove, Agdaagux Tribe, King Cove Corporation, and Aleutians East Borough believe that a cost-efficient, reliable surface transportation system, specifically a road, is needed between the City of King Cove and Cold Bay Airport. The transportation system must be affordable for local families, and be constructed, operated, and maintained at a cost that can be borne by local or state government. The transportation must be practical in the context of the Cold Bay and King Cove area, so that it can be operated and maintained without undue requirements for specially trained personnel or specialized equipment, and can provide safe, reliable, affordable transportation with the least amount of interruption by weather conditions.

ES-1.4   Alternatives

The Service evaluated five alternatives in the EIS, guided by the purpose and need, the Act, and NEPA. The Act directs the Secretary of Interior to prepare an EIS that will analyze the impacts of a proposed land exchange with the State of Alaska and the King Cove Corporation for the purpose of construction and operation of a road between the communities of King Cove and Cold Bay, Alaska.

- The Act requires the analysis of at least one road alternative that is developed in consultation with the State of Alaska, the City of King Cove, and the Agdaagux Tribe of King Cove.

- The Act specifies several elements to minimize adverse impacts of the road corridor on adjacent refuge lands, including a cable barrier on each side of the road, unless a different barrier type is required by the Record of Decision for the EIS; transferring the minimum acreage of federal land required for the construction of a road corridor; and incorporating roads that are in existence. Mitigation elements identified in the Act include the avoidance of wildlife impacts and mitigation of wetland loss, and the development of an enforceable mitigation plan.

- NEPA requires documentation of the alternative development process, including alternatives considered but dismissed from further analysis.

- NEPA requires the analysis of a No Action alternative and the analysis of a reasonable range of alternatives.

Alternative 1 – No Action

Under Alternative 1, the Service would not enter into a land exchange with King Cove Corporation and the State of Alaska for the purpose of constructing a road between King Cove and Cold Bay, Alaska. Current modes of transportation between the cities of King Cove and Cold Bay would continue to operate, including air, personal marine vessels, ferry service approximately twice per month in the summer season, and seasonal hovercraft service. This alternative assumes that The Aleutians East Borough would reinstitute hovercraft service between the new northeast terminal and Cross Wind Cove in 2013. Scheduled hovercraft service would be three days per week during the months of April through October.

As the Draft EIS was approaching completion, the Aleutians East Borough sent the Service a letter stating that they will not resume hovercraft service in the foreseeable future. Due to the timing of the letter, we are unable to restructure the analysis of consequences to reflect this change in the No Action alternative in the Draft EIS. While the Borough does not plan to operate the hovercraft, all other aspects of the No Action alternative remain the same. The Final EIS will reflect this change and other changes that are made in response to public comments.

Alternative 2 – Land Exchange and Southern Road Alignment

Alternative 2 proposes a land exchange between the federal government, State of Alaska, and King Cove Corporation as described in the Proposed Action. The estimated amount of federal land exchanged in this alternative for the road corridor would be 201 acres, including 131 acres in Izembek Wilderness, assuming a 100-foot corridor width.

Under this alternative, the Service would execute an administrative boundary adjustment in the vicinity of Blinn Lake, in accord with the *Alaska National Interest Lands Conservation Act* (ANILCA) Section 103(b). An area that is currently designated as Alaska Peninsula National Wildlife Refuge, but administered by Izembek National Wildlife Refuge, would become part of Izembek National Wildlife Refuge (Figure ES-2).

Figure ES-2 Proposed National Wildlife Refuge Boundary Adjustment

The southern road alignment (Figure ES-3, Alternative 2) would originate at the terminus of the King Cove Access Road (currently under construction) in the vicinity of the Northeast Hovercraft Terminal. The initial 6 miles would be co-located with the central alignment (Alternative 3). The southern alignment would cross 2 fish bearing streams, and continue along gently rolling hills. At a point 6 miles north of the Northeast Hovercraft Terminal, the southern alignment would depart from the central alignment in a westerly direction, and stay south of the ridge line that separates the watersheds of the Kinzarof and Izembek lagoons. The alignment would continue westerly, avoiding lakes, and crossing 6 more fish bearing streams. At about 12.4 miles from the start, the southern alignment would again be co-located with the central alignment and follow Outpost Trail (which transitions to Outpost Road) in a southwesterly direction to a point just north of Blinn Lake. At that point, the southern alignment would depart from the central alignment, following an existing primitive road for approximately 1.4 miles around the east and south side of Blinn Lake to intersect with Outer Marker Road (Figure ES-3, Alternative 2). The route would continue south along Outer Marker Road to its intersection with St. Louis Road, and then follow St. Louis Road to terminate at the refuge/state boundary.

The portion of the alignment that is exclusive to the southern alignment (not co-located with the central alignment) would be located only in the watershed of Kinzarof Lagoon. The co-located alignment would be located in the watersheds of Izembek and Kinzarof lagoons. The road corridor would be located approximately ½ mile to 1 mile north of Kinzarof Lagoon. This alignment is intended to strike a compromise between minimizing disturbance to Black Brant (through distance from Kinzarof Lagoon) and disrupting caribou migration through the isthmus. The route was designed to avoid or minimize impacts to wetlands, minimize stream crossings, and to accommodate terrain considerations.

The values used in the comparison of Alternatives 2 and 3 including the number and type of drainage structures, fill quantities, and typical roadway sections and design details presented in tables and figures are estimates calculated for analysis purposes. Final project design and construction details may be different. Additional design criteria are discussed in the Draft EIS.

The road for Alternative 2 would be classified as a Rural Minor Collector, with rolling terrain and a design speed of 20 miles per hour. It would be a single-lane gravel road with turn-outs. The road would include a barrier along both sides of the roadway to prevent vehicles from accessing the Izembek National Wildlife Refuge and Izembek Wilderness lands adjacent to the road. Table ES-1 shows the characteristics of Alternative 2 and Alternative 3 roadways.

Figure ES-3 Alternative 2 – Southern Road Alignment

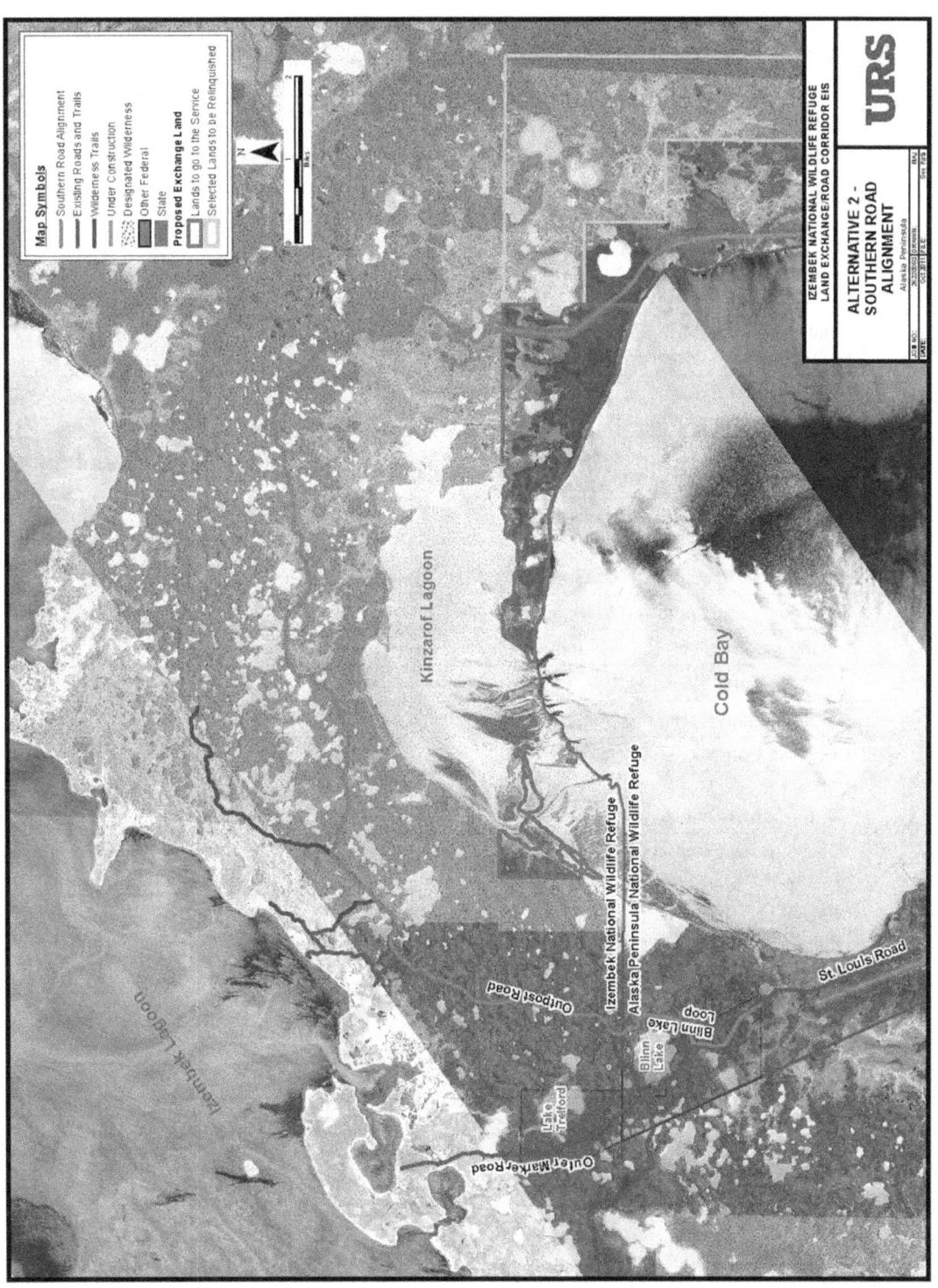

IZEMBEK NATIONAL WILDLIFE REFUGE
LAND EXCHANGE/ROAD CORRIDOR EIS

Table ES-1 Comparative Summary of Road Alternatives

	Alternative 2: Land Exchange and Southern Road Alignment	Alternative 3: Land Exchange and Central Road Alignment
Road Corridor in Acres, Assuming 100-Foot Width	236	262
Total Length of Corridor (miles)	19.4	21.6
Road Corridor in Acres Proposed for Exchange from National Wildlife Refuge	201	227
Road Corridor in Miles Proposed for Exchange from National Wildlife Refuge	16.5	18.7
Road Corridor in Acres Proposed for Exchange from Izembek Wilderness	131	152
Road Corridor in Miles Proposed for Exchange from Izembek Wilderness	10.8	12.5
Road Corridor in Acres on Lands Owned by King Cove Corporation	35	35
Road Corridor in Miles on Lands Owned by King Cove Corporation	2.9	2.9
Total Road Footprint of New Construction in Acres	107	100
Average Road Footprint Width in Feet	47.6	41.4
Maximum Road Footprint Width in Feet	91	92
Minimum Road Footprint Width in Feet	30	30
Width of Traffic Lane in Feet	13	13
Width of Safety Turnout in Feet	11	11
Miles of Road Construction	18.5	20.0
Miles of Road Constructed/Reconstructed on Existing Roads/Trails	6.0	9.0
Miles of Road Constructed on Lands with No Previous Road	12.5	11.0
Miles of Existing Road in Exchange Corridor Requiring No Construction	0.9	1.6
Number of Turnouts for Passing	136	158
Drainage Structures	162	173
Bridges	1	1
Culverts or Bridges	7	1
Cross Culverts (Pipes)	154	171
Material Site(s)[*]	1	1
Total Fill Quantity in Cubic Yards	256,000	302,000
Fill Quantity from Material Site in Cubic Yards	182,000	231,000
Material Site Footprint in Acres	6	7

	Alternative 2: Land Exchange and Southern Road Alignment	Alternative 3: Land Exchange and Central Road Alignment
Acres of Wetlands Filled for Road Construction	3.8	2.4
Quantity of Fill in Wetlands for Road Construction in Cubic Yards	20,000 to 25,000	11,000 to 15,000
Disposal Sites	0	0
Quantity of Unusable Excavated Material in Cubic Yards	0	0
Acres of Uplands Reclaimed with Excavated Material	0.3	2.4
Temporary Barge Landing Sites	2	2
Area of Barge Landing Site in Acres	0.5	0.5
Acres of State Tidelands in Barge Landing Site	Less than 0.1	Less than 0.1
Fill Quantity for Barge Landing Site Development in Cubic Yards	1,200	1,200
Fill Quantity Below High Tide Line in Cubic Yards	1,000	1,000
Upland Fill Quantity in Cubic Yards	200	200

Note: *One site identified; if that site is not sufficient, other sites may be located in the future to generate the same estimated quantity on private lands.

Alternative 3 – Land Exchange and Central Road Alignment

Alternative 3 proposes a land exchange between the federal government, State of Alaska, and King Cove Corporation, as described in the Proposed Action. The estimated amount of federal land exchanged in this alternative for the road corridor would be 227 acres, including 152 acres in Izembek Wilderness, assuming a 100-foot corridor width.

Under this alternative, the Service would execute an administrative boundary adjustment in the vicinity of Blinn Lake, in accord with ANILCA Section 103(b). An area that is currently designated as Alaska Peninsula National Wildlife Refuge, but administered by Izembek National Wildlife Refuge, would become part of Izembek National Wildlife Refuge (Figure ES-2).

The central road alignment (Figure ES-4, Alternative 3) would originate at the terminus of the King Cove Access Road (currently under construction) in the vicinity of the Northeast Hovercraft Terminal. The initial 6 miles would be co-located with the southern alignment (Alternative 2). The alignment would cross 2 fish bearing streams, and continue along gently rolling hills. At a point 6 miles north of the Northeast Hovercraft Terminal, the central alignment would depart from the southern alignment and wind north and then westerly through steep hills and around lakes of the isthmus divide to Outpost Trail. The alignment would be co-located with the southern alignment, along Outpost Trail (which transitions to Outpost Road) to an intersection north of Blinn Lake. The central alignment would depart from the southern alignment north of Blinn Lake, continuing along Outpost Road to intersect with Outer Marker Road to the west of Blinn Lake. The route would continue south along Outer Marker Road to intersect with St. Louis Road, terminating at the refuge/state boundary.

The central alignment would be located in the watersheds of Izembek and Kinzarof lagoons. The alignment was designed to avoid or minimize impacts to wetlands and high value habitat for breeding, nesting, and migrating waterbirds, to reduce disturbance or impacts to species and habitat in both Izembek and Kinzarof lagoons, while also considering land mammal (caribou, bear, furbearers) movement and habitat use of the isthmus. This alignment seeks to minimize impacts to wetlands and lake-dependent resources, avoid or minimize stream crossings, and to accommodate terrain considerations.

The values used in the comparison of Alternatives 2 and 3, including the number and type of drainage structures, fill quantities, and typical roadway sections and design details presented in tables and figures are estimates calculated for analysis purposes. Final project design and construction details may be different.

The road for Alternative 3 would be classified as a Rural Minor Collector, with rolling terrain and a design speed of 20 miles per hour. It would be a single-lane gravel road with turn-outs. The road would include a barrier along both sides of the roadway to prevent vehicles from accessing the Izembek National Wildlife Refuge and Izembek Wilderness lands adjacent to the road.

Figure ES-4 Alternative 3 – Central Road Alignment

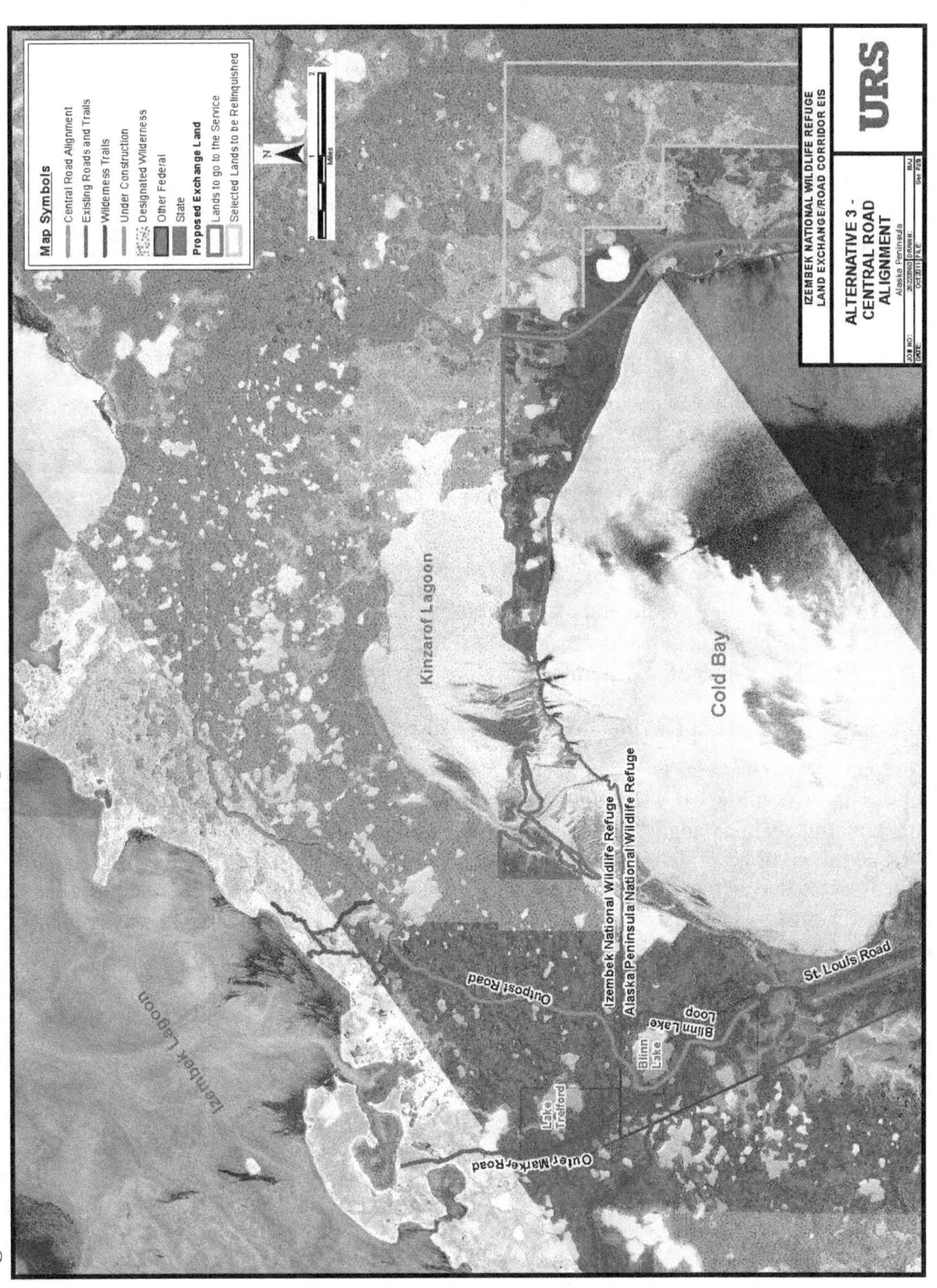

Alternative 4 – Hovercraft Operations from the Northeast Hovercraft Terminal to Cross Wind Cove (Six days per week)

Alternative 4 is the Proposed Action in the 2003 EIS. This alternative, as proposed in the 2003 EIS, has not been fully implemented to date. However, actions authorized by the Record of Decision are ongoing. Continued activities for development of the access road and the Northeast Hovercraft Terminal were contracted in 2011 for construction in 2012. The alternative considered in this EIS would not require further construction activities; the alternative will consider operations of the hovercraft, as described in the 2003 EIS, for service 6 days per week between the Northeast Hovercraft Terminal and the Cross Wind Cove (Figure ES-5, Alternative 4).

As the Draft EIS was approaching completion, the Aleutians East Borough sent the Service a letter stating that they will not resume hovercraft service in the foreseeable future. Alternative 4 does not assume that the Borough is the operator of this alternative, only that the existing hovercraft would be used. All other aspects of the alternative remain the same. The Final EIS will reflect this change and other changes that are made in response to public comments.

Alternative 4 would be located on lands owned by King Cove Corporation and the State of Alaska. A land exchange would not occur, though lands previously selected within Izembek Wilderness by the King Cove Corporation under ANSCA would eventually be conveyed.

Alternative 4 consists of the following major components:

- Use existing hovercraft and existing terminal at Cross Wind Cove
- Completion of contract to construct Northeast Hovercraft Terminal and access road
- No additional ground disturbing activities beyond what was identified in the 2003 EIS.

Alternative 5 – Lenard Harbor Ferry with Cold Bay Dock Improvements

Alternative 5 would use a ferry to travel 14 miles between a terminal in Lenard Harbor and a substantially modified Cold Bay dock (Figure ES-6, Alternative 5). This alternative is similar to an alternative that was analyzed in the 2003 EIS, with the exception of project elements that have been permitted or constructed to date, including the access road to the site, a terminal building with associated utility infrastructure, and a parking area. However, the Lenard Harbor terminal structure has been damaged by a storm, and would have to be replaced. Upgrades to the parking area and security fencing would also be necessary. Ferry service would be provided 6 days per week.

Alternative 5 would be located on lands owned by King Cove Corporation, The Aleut Corporation, and the State of Alaska. A land exchange would not occur, though lands previously selected within Izembek Wilderness by the King Cove Corporation under ANSCA would eventually be conveyed.

Figure ES-5 Alternative 4 (Hovercraft from Northeast Hovercraft Terminal)

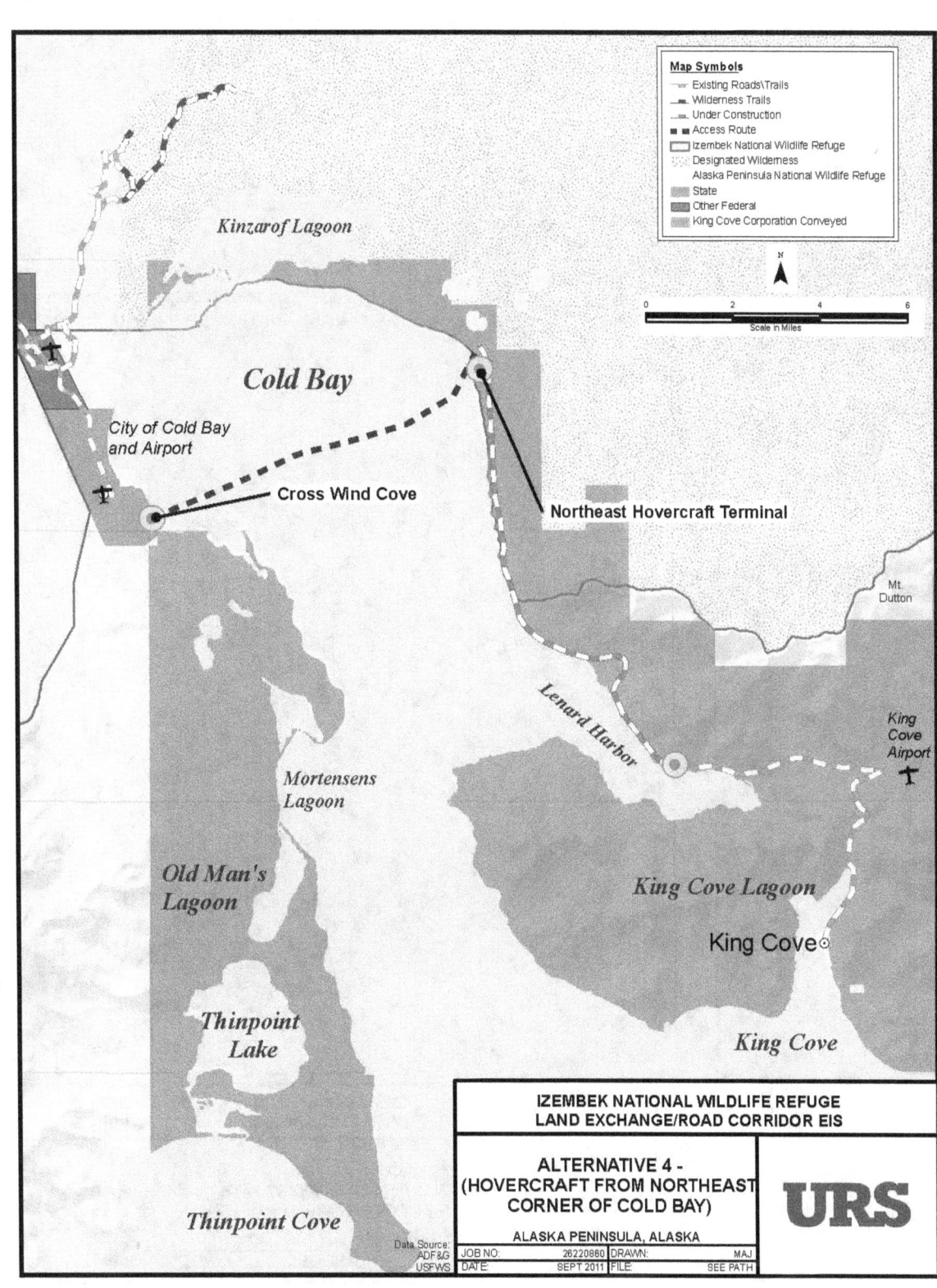

Figure ES-6 Alternative 5 (Lenard Harbor Ferry with Cold Bay Dock Improvements)

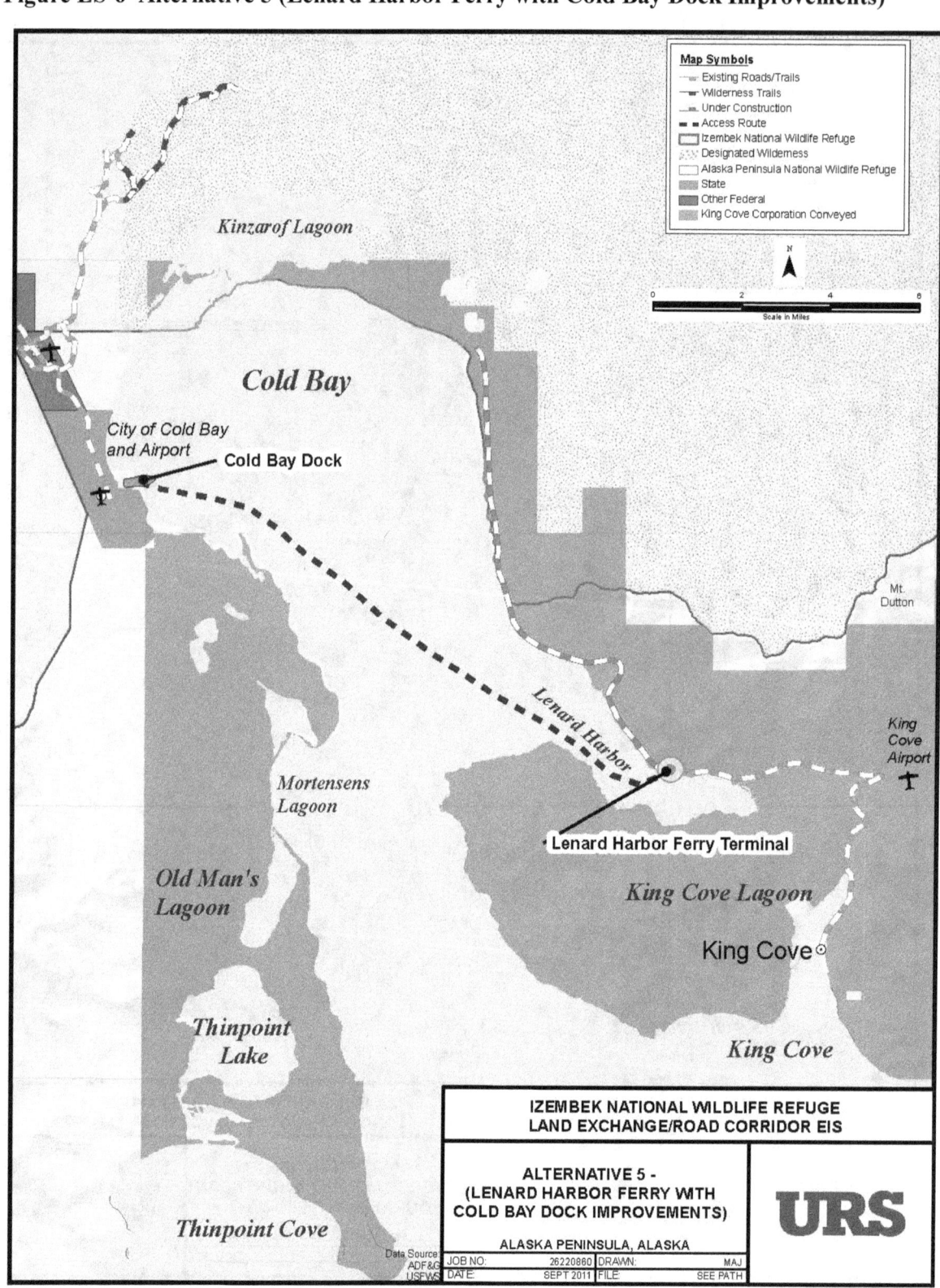

Alternative 5 consists of the following major components:

- Lenard Harbor ferry dock and terminal
- Major modification of the existing Cold Bay dock by adding a wave barrier, vehicle ramp system for on- and off-loading vehicles at water level, and a pedestrian walkway
- A displacement monohull, open deck ferry with ice-breaking capabilities
- One material site, one disposal site for unusable excavated materials, and one temporary barge landing site/staging area required for construction.

ES-1.5   Comparison of Alternatives

Table ES-2 shows a summary of the five alternatives, including cost. Lands potentially affected by the proposed project are summarized in Tables ES-3 and ES-4. Complete descriptions of the exchange parcels are included in Appendix B of the Draft EIS.

Six parcels are involved in the proposed land exchange under Alternatives 2 and 3. Upon completion of the land exchange proposed under Alternatives 2 or 3, Izembek State Game Refuge would also include state lands and water in the vicinity of Kinzarof Lagoon, in accord with the *Izembek State Game Refuge Land Exchange Bill*.

Alternatives 4 and 5 would not include a land exchange, but would potentially affect 3 parcels. In addition, the lands selected by King Cove Corporation within Izembek Wilderness would eventually be conveyed to the Corporation if Alternative 4 or 5 were implemented.

Table ES-2 Comparative Summary of Alternatives

	Alternative 1: No Action	Alternative 2: Land Exchange and Southern Road Alignment	Alternative 3: Land Exchange and Central Road Alignment	Alternative 4: Hovercraft Operations (No Land Exchange)	Alternative 5: Lenard Harbor Ferry with Cold Bay Dock Improvements (No Land Exchange)
New Footprint in Acres	0	107	100	0	1.9
Acres Removed from Izembek Wilderness	5,430 (selected lands)	131 (road corridor)	152 (road corridor)	5,430 (selected lands)	5,430 (selected lands)
Acres Added to Wilderness	0	44,491 (includes State parcel and Kinzarof parcel)	44,491 (includes State parcel and Kinzarof parcel)	0	0
Acres of Land Selection Relinquished in Wilderness	0	5,430	5,430	0	0
Estimated Area of Exchange Parcel for Road Corridor	0	201	227	0	0
Acres Removed from Alaska Maritime National Wildlife Refuge (Sitkinak Island)		1,619	1,619		
New Acres of Wetlands Filled on Corporation Lands		1.1	1.1		0.4
New Acres of Wetlands Filled on Wilderness Lands		2.7	1.3		
New Acres of Wetlands Filled on Refuge Lands (not Wilderness)		0	0		
Total New Acres of Wetlands Filled	0	3.8	2.4	0	0.4
Construction Cost in Millions	0	$20.7	$22.7	0	$27.1
Maintenance/ Annual Operation Costs	$1.0 Million	$149,000	$158,000	$2.0 Million	$2.3 Million
Lifecycle Cost in Millions	$26.3	$23.4	$25.7	$44.4	$70.2

Table ES-3 Land Exchange Parcels under Alternatives 2 and 3

Parcel	Current Surface Owner	Current Subsurface Owner	Estimated Area (Acres)	Current Management Regime
Road Corridor	Federal –Service and Federal Aviation Administration	Federal	201± Alt 2 227± Alt 3	Wilderness and National Wildlife Refuge; Withdrawal for Federal Aviation Administration
Sitkinak Island	Federal – Coast Guard and Service	Federal	1,619±	Airstrip, Coast Guard Base
State Lands	State – Department of Natural Resources	State	41,887±	General Use
Mortensens Lagoon	Native Corporation – King Cove Corporation	Native Corporation – The Aleut Corporation	8,092±	Private
Kinzarof Lagoon	Native Corporation – King Cove Corporation	Federal	2,604±	Private
King Cove Corporation Selected Lands	Federal – King Cove Corporation Selection	Federal	5,430±	Wilderness

Table ES-4 Lands Potentially Affected under Alternatives 4 and 5

Parcel	Current Surface Owner	Current Subsurface Owner	Area (Acres)	Current Management Regime
Northeast Hovercraft Terminal Site	King Cove Corporation, State	State	No new footprint	Private; construction site
Lenard Harbor Ferry Terminal Site	King Cove Corporation, State	The Aleut Corporation, State	0.5	Private
Cold Bay Dock Site	State	State	Less than 0.1 acre	Public Dock (owned by Aleutians East Borough)
King Cove Corporation Selected Lands	Federal – King Cove Corporation Selection	Federal	5,430±	Wilderness

ES-1.6   Summary of Impacts

The impact criteria for direct and indirect, and cumulative effects are:

- Intensity – the magnitude of change in the resource condition
- Duration – how long would a change last
- Extent – the geographic area would be affected
- Context –rare or protected resources that would be affected.

The summary ratings shown for each resource are:

- No Effect – the alternative would not affect resources
- Negligible – generally low intensity, temporary, local, and do not affect unique resources
- Minor – generally low intensity, temporary, local, although common resources may have more intense longer term impacts
- Moderate –common and important resources may have higher impact levels and unique resources may have lower impact levels
- Major – generally medium or high intensity, long term or permanent, regional or extended, and important or unique

Table ES-5 shows a graphic summary of direct and indirect effects for each alternative, by resource. Table ES-6 shows a narrative summary of direct, indirect, and cumulative impacts for each alternative, by resource. The following paragraphs provide a brief narrative overview of generalized impact analysis conclusions.

Alternative 1 – No Action

Effects would generally be negligible to minor, except for moderate effects to fiscal resources, analyzed as a component of socioeconomics. The effects to fiscal resources include the cost for operation of the hovercraft, which would continue to require an annual subsidy of approximately $1 million. The negligible to minor effects to other resources would be from ongoing operations of the hovercraft and the eventual conveyance approximately 5,430 acres in Izembek Wilderness to King Cove Corporation selected under ANCSA. King Cove Corporation's right to select the parcel in Izembek Wilderness pre-dates the establishment of the wilderness. Effects from hovercraft operations have both beneficial and adverse effects. Startle response in animals is an example of a minor adverse effect of hovercraft operations. Reinstituting a seasonal hovercraft service for medical evacuation is an incremental addition to existing aircraft transportation, and although not optimal, this improvement in public health and transportation options in the region may be considered a minor beneficial effect.

Alternative 2 – Land Exchange and Southern Road Alignment and Alternative 3 – Land Exchange and Central Road Alignment

The analysis of impacts for Alternatives 2 and 3 are very similar. While there is some variation in the potential impacts based on the different alignments, both alternatives would have major effects to public health and safety, transportation, land ownership and use, wilderness, public use, cultural resources, fish and essential fish habitat, and birds. The major beneficial effects to public health and safety and transportation would include increased opportunity for people in the City of King Cove to travel to the Cold Bay Airport for access to specialized medical services. The road alternatives would result in distinctive changes transportation options, patterns, and costs, and add a full-time transportation link between the communities of King Cove and Cold Bay.

The proposed exchange of federal, state, and King Cove Corporation lands would have a major adverse impact to Izembek Wilderness; approximately 131 acres would be removed from Izembek Wilderness under Alternative 2 and 152 acres would be removed under Alternative 3 for the respective road corridor, which would fragment the wilderness and impact natural quality, undeveloped quality, and opportunities for solitude. Approximately 44,491 acres would be added to Alaska Peninsula National Wildlife Refuge as wilderness under either alternative, which would be a major beneficial effect.

The land exchange would affect land ownership and public use on the parcels previously managed as state or private land which would become wilderness or national wildlife refuge. These major effects are considered neither adverse nor beneficial.

Ground disturbing activities associated with construction of the road in increased access into previously unroaded areas could have a moderate to major adverse impact on archaeological sites. Increased harvesting pressure on streams could result from increased access, which could have a major adverse effect on fish resources. Road construction and operation would have a major adverse effect on Tundra Swan, Brant, Emporer Goose and Common Loon populations, and a moderate effect on other breeding birds, migrating birds, and wintering birds. In addition, Alternative 2 would have a major adverse effect on caribou. Alternatives 2 and 3 would have a moderate adverse effect on bears.

Alternative 4 – Hovercraft Operations from the Northeast Hovercraft Terminal to Cross Wind Cove (Six days per week)

The effects from implementation of Alternative 4 would generally be negligible to minor; however, effects to fiscal resources and public health and safety would be major, and effects to transportation and wilderness would be moderate. The major adverse effects to fiscal resources would include the cost for operation of the hovercraft, which would continue to require an annual subsidy of approximately $2 million. The major beneficial effects to public health and safety and the moderate beneficial effects to transportation would result from regularly scheduled year-round transportation from the City of King Cove to the Cold Bay Airport, and the availability of the hovercraft for most emergency medical evacuations. Minor to moderate adverse effects to wilderness would result from increased hovercraft operations; intermittent noise or visual disturbances would occur in localized areas, which would affect wilderness qualities.

Negligible to minor adverse effects to other resources would be similar to Alternative 1, resulting from ongoing operations of the hovercraft and the eventual conveyance approximately 5,430 acres in Izembek Wilderness to King Cove Corporation selected under ANCSA.

Alternative 5 – Lenard Harbor Ferry with Cold Bay Dock Improvements

Effects from implementation of Alternative 5 would be similar to Alternative 4 in that there would be major effects to fiscal resources and public health and safety, moderate effects to transportation, and negligible to minor effects to other resources. The major adverse effects to fiscal resources would include the cost for operation of the ferry, which would require an annual subsidy of approximately $2.3 million. The major beneficial effects to public health and safety and the moderate beneficial effects to transportation would result from regularly scheduled year-round transportation from the City of King Cove to the Cold Bay dock, and the availability of the ferry for most emergency medical evacuations. Negligible to minor adverse effects to other resources would include impacts associated with the construction and new footprint of the Lenard Harbor ferry terminal, improvements to the Cold Bay dock, and disturbance due to operations of the ferry.

Table ES-5 Summary of Direct and Indirect Impacts

	Alternative 1 No Action	Alternative 2 Land Exchange and Southern Road Alignment	Alternative 3 Land Exchange and Central Road Alignment	Alternative 4 Hovercraft Operations from the Northeast Terminal	Alternative 5 Lenard Harbor Ferry with Cold Bay Dock Improvements
Air Quality	Ne	Minor	Minor	Ne	Minor
Climate	Ne	Ne	Ne	Ne	Ne
Geology	Ne	Moderate	Moderate	Ne	Minor
Hydrology	Ne	Moderate	Moderate	Ne	Ne
Hazardous Materials	Ne	Moderate	Moderate	Ne	Ne
Noise	Ne	Minor	Minor	Ne	Ne
Terrestrial and Aquatic Plant Communities	No effect	Moderate	Moderate	Minor	Minor
Wetlands	No effect	Moderate	Moderate	No effect	Minor
Fish and Essential Fish Habitat	Ne	Major	Major	Ne	Ne
Birds	Minor	Minor-Major, by species	Minor-Major, by species	Minor	Minor
Land Mammals	Minor	Minor-Moderate, by species	Minor-Moderate, by species	Minor	Minor
Marine Mammals	Minor	Minor	Minor	Minor	Minor
Threatened & Endangered Species	Minor	No effect-Moderate, by species	No effect-Moderate, by species	Minor	Minor
Land Use	Minor	Major	Major	Minor	Minor
Socioeconomic	Moderate	Moderate	Moderate	Major	Major
Transportation	Minor	Major	Major	Moderate	Moderate
Public Health & Safety	Minor	Major	Major	Major	Major
Environmental Justice	No adverse effect	No adverse effect	No adverse effect	No adverse effect	No adverse effect
Public Use	Ne	Major	Major	Ne	Ne
Subsistence	No effect	Minor	Minor	Ne	Ne
Cultural Resources	No effect	Major	Major	No effect	Minor
Visual	Ne	Moderate	Moderate	Ne	Minor
Wilderness	Minor	Major	Major	Moderate	Minor

If a range of impacts is given in the text, the highest value is represented.
Ne = Negligible

Table ES-6 Direct, Indirect, and Cumulative Effects by Alternative and Resource

	Alternative 1: No Action - Existing Air and Marine Service	Alternative 2: Land Exchange and Southern Road Alignment	Alternative 3: Land Exchange and Central Road Alignment	Alternative 4: Hovercraft Operations from the Northeast Hovercraft Terminal to Cross Wind Cove 6 days per Week	Alternative 5: Lenard Harbor Ferry with Cold Bay Dock Improvement
Air Quality					
Overall Effects	The total estimated annual emissions would consist of small emission sources, operating intermittently, and spread out over a relatively large area. The effects would be *negligible*.	This alternative would reduce emissions from hovercraft operations to zero, but would contribute to an overall increase in emissions. The total estimated annual emissions would consist of small emission sources, operating intermittently, and spread out over a relatively large area. Overall effects to air quality would be *minor*.	Effects on air quality would be similar to Alternative 2. *minor*.	There would be negligible direct effects on air quality in the immediate vicinity of the hovercraft. The total estimated annual emissions would consist of small emission sources, operating intermittently, and spread out over a relatively large area. The overall effect would be *negligible*.	There would be effects on air quality in the immediate vicinity of the ferry. The total estimated annual emissions would consist of small emission sources, operating intermittently, and spread out over a relatively large area. The overall effect on air quality would be *negligible to minor*.
Cumulative Effects	New sources of emissions by 2013 would include possible construction dust from Cold Bay Airport improvements, and traffic on a completed road to the Northeast Hovercraft Terminal. Operation of the hovercraft would have a *negligible* contribution to cumulative effects.	Increases in road traffic would shift from other modes of travel. The contribution of this alternative to cumulative effects would be *minor*.	The contribution to cumulative effects would be similar to Alternative 2. *minor*.	Activities that have the potential to emit air pollution in the area around the hovercraft operations (boat traffic, aircraft passes, and vehicles, for example) are already included in the background, or ambient air, which is expected to meet air quality standards. The contribution to cumulative effects would be *negligible*.	Activities that have the potential to emit air pollution in the area around the ferry operations (boat traffic, aircraft passes, and vehicles, for example) are already included in the background, or ambient air, which is expected to meet air quality standards. The contribution of this alternative to cumulative effects is would be *negligible*.

	Alternative 1: No Action - Existing Air and Marine Service	Alternative 2: Land Exchange and Southern Road Alignment	Alternative 3: Land Exchange and Central Road Alignment	Alternative 4: Hovercraft Operations from the Northeast Hovercraft Terminal to Cross Wind Cove 6 days per Week	Alternative 5: Lenard Harbor Ferry with Cold Bay Dock Improvement
Climate					
Overall Effects	The estimated total of 620 tons per year of carbon dioxide emissions is not expected to be perceptible, and the effect to climate from Alternative 1 would be *negligible*.	The estimated total of 877 tons per year of carbon dioxide emissions is not expected to be perceptible, and the effect to climate from Alternative 2 would be *negligible*.	The estimated total of 912 tons per year of carbon dioxide emissions is not expected to be perceptible, and the effect to climate from Alternative 3 effects would be *negligible*.	The estimated total of 2,075 tons per year of carbon dioxide emissions is not expected to be perceptible, and the effect to climate from Alternative 4 would be *negligible*.	The estimated total of 938 tons per year of carbon dioxide emissions is not expected to be perceptible, and the effect to climate from Alternative 5 would be *negligible*.
Cumulative Effects	Global climate change effects currently have a high enough intensity that perceptible changes around the globe have occurred. When compared to other global actions, Alternative 1 is expected to have a *negligible* contribution to cumulative effects.	The contribution to cumulative effects would be similar to Alternative 1, *negligible*.	The contribution to cumulative effects would be similar to Alternative 1, *negligible*.	The contribution to cumulative effects would be similar to Alternative 1, *negligible*.	The contribution to cumulative effects would be similar to Alternative 1, *negligible*.
Geology and Soils					
Overall Effects	*Negligible to minor* effects may include shoreline erosion from wave action generated by the hovercraft during departures and arrivals, and refueling on land.	Though impacts from Alternative 2 would be reduced in the period following the project completion, construction would disturb a total of 107 acres of surface and shallow subsurface soil along the road corridor and 0.5 acres at a construction staging area near the Northeast Hovercraft Terminal. Approximately 111,000 cubic yards of geologic resource material would be excavated during cut and fill activities. The effect would be *moderate*.	Effects of Alternative 3 would be similar to those in Alternative 2, disturbing a total of 100 acres of surface and shallow subsurface soil along the road corridor and 0.5 acres at a construction staging area near the Northeast Hovercraft Terminal. Approximately 99,000 cubic yards of geologic resource material would be excavated during cut and fill activities. The effect would be *moderate*.	Effects may include shoreline erosion from wave action generated by the hovercraft during departures and arrivals, and refueling on land. Because the hovercraft would operate more often than in Alternative 1, the effect would be *negligible to minor*.	There would be *no effects* on geology and soils from operation and maintenance of a ferry. *Minor* effects would occur due to dock construction activities, because of the disturbance to submerged sediments as a result of dredging and pile driving.

	Alternative 1: No Action - Existing Air and Marine Service	Alternative 2: Land Exchange and Southern Road Alignment	Alternative 3: Land Exchange and Central Road Alignment	Alternative 4: Hovercraft Operations from the Northeast Hovercraft Terminal to Cross Wind Cove 6 days per Week	Alternative 5: Lenard Harbor Ferry with Cold Bay Dock Improvement
Cumulative Effects	The continuing effects from the operation of the hovercraft 3 days per week, April through October, would have a *negligible* contribution to cumulative effects on geology and soils in the EIS project area.	The resulting erosion of soil in areas disturbed by construction or staging could lead to water channelization of runoff, and would add to existing effects on geology and soil resources. The cumulative effect would be *moderate*.	Cumulative effects would be similar to those discussed under Alternative 2, *moderate*.	Cumulative effects would be the same as described under Alternative 1. Although the frequency of hovercraft operations under this alternative would be greater, the incremental addition to cumulative effects would remain *negligible*.	There would be negligible incremental additions to cumulative effects as a result of construction activities on less than 1 acre at the Lenard Harbor site. Cumulative effects would be the same as described under Alternative 1, *negligible*.
Hydrology					
Overall Effects	Impacts to water resources and water quality related to Alternative 1 would result in *negligible* effects. These effects may include fuel and sewage releases at the docking locations and along the preferred routes.	Effects to hydrologic processes would occur as a result of fill placement in approximately 3.8 acres of wetland, and the installation of an estimated 162 drainage structures along the road. The uncontained release of hazardous materials and from stream turbidity generated by streambank construction activities could also occur. The increase in sediment load from road runoff would impact the quality of water bodies which are considered essential fish habitat. The effect would be *moderate*.	Effects to hydrologic processes would occur as a result of fill placement in approximately 2.4 acres of wetland, and the installation of an estimated 173 drainage structures along the road. The uncontained release of hazardous materials and from stream turbidity generated by streambank construction activities could also occur. The increase in sediment load from road runoff would impact the quality of water bodies which are considered essential fish habitat. The effect would be *moderate*.	Impacts to water resources and water quality related to the implementation of Alternative 4 would result in *negligible* effects. These effects may include fuel and sewage releases at the docking locations and along the preferred routes.	The greatest impacts to water quality include increase in turbidity due to dredging and pile driving activities at the Lenard Harbor ferry terminal and modifications at the Cold Bay Dock and refueling of the ferry in open-water at the Cold Bay dock. As construction would be limited to less than 1 acre adjacent to the existing hovercraft site, activities would have *negligible* effects on hydrologic processes within the project area. Effects from operation and maintenance of a ferry could include effects from the release of hazardous materials such as fuel, battery acid or hydraulic fluid, which would also be *negligible*.

	Alternative 1: No Action – Existing Air and Marine Service	Alternative 2: Land Exchange and Southern Road Alignment	Alternative 3: Land Exchange and Central Road Alignment	Alternative 4: Hovercraft Operations from the Northeast Hovercraft Terminal to Cross Wind Cove 6 days per Week	Alternative 5: Lenard Harbor Ferry with Cold Bay Dock Improvement
Cumulative Effects	The continuing effects from the operation of the hovercraft 3 days per week, April through October, would have a *negligible* contribution to cumulative effects on hydrology and hydrologic processes in the EIS project area.	Long-term maintenance of stream crossings would be additive to those impacts derived during construction activities. Effects could include potential non-point source pollution and unlawful stream crossings along the margins of the road corridor by the general public. Effects would be *moderate*.	Effects as a result of the land exchange and construction under Alternative 3 are similar to those described under Alternative 2, *moderate*.	Cumulative effects would be the same as described under Alternative 1. Although the frequency of hovercraft operations under this alternative would be greater, the incremental addition to cumulative effects would remain *negligible*.	There would be *negligible* incremental additions to cumulative effects on water resources and water quality within Cold Bay. The impacts from ferry vessels may include fuel and sewage releases at the docking locations and along the preferred routes of the ferry vessels.

Hazardous Materials

	Alternative 1: No Action – Existing Air and Marine Service	Alternative 2: Land Exchange and Southern Road Alignment	Alternative 3: Land Exchange and Central Road Alignment	Alternative 4: Hovercraft Operations from the Northeast Hovercraft Terminal to Cross Wind Cove 6 days per Week	Alternative 5: Lenard Harbor Ferry with Cold Bay Dock Improvement
Overall Effects	The hovercraft operations would have *negligible* impacts regarding hazardous materials. Fuel spills are a low probability event, but could affect water quality.	Effects from hazardous materials could occur during construction from the uncontrolled release of fuel, battery acid or hydraulic fluid, though it is of low probability with proper handling. Effects would be *minor to moderate*.	Effects of Alternative 3 are similar to those described under Alternative 2, *minor to moderate*.	The hovercraft operations would have *negligible* impacts regarding hazardous materials. Fuel spills are a low probability event, but could affect water quality.	During operations no re-suspension of the contaminated sediments in marine waters would be expected, but this would occur during dock construction. The ferry would be refueled over water at the Cold Bay dock which would present a risk of a fuel spill of hazardous materials. The overall effect is considered *negligible*.
Cumulative Effects	This alternative would have a *negligible* contribution to cumulative effects on the management of hazardous materials.	There are no foreseeable future actions in the immediate vicinity that would affect the management of hazardous materials. A fuel spill on land would have a *minor* cumulative effect to existing uses and a *moderate* cumulative effect if it occurred in wetlands or a water body.	Effects as a result of the land exchange and construction under Alternative 3 are similar to those described under Alternative 2, *minor to moderate*.	This alternative would have a *negligible* contribution to cumulative effects on water quality.	The land exchange would not be implemented; thus there are no impacts regarding the transfer of responsibility of contaminated sites. There would be *negligible* incremental additions to cumulative effects as a result of construction or operation activities on less than 1 acre at the Lenard Harbor site.

Noise

	Alternative 1: No Action – Existing Air and Marine Service	Alternative 2: Land Exchange and Southern Road Alignment	Alternative 3: Land Exchange and Central Road Alignment	Alternative 4: Hovercraft Operations from the Northeast Hovercraft Terminal to Cross Wind Cove 6 days per Week	Alternative 5: Lenard Harbor Ferry with Cold Bay Dock Improvement
Overall Effects	There would be no new noise generating activities under Alternative 1. The noise effects, at 65 dBA at 1,000 feet from the operation of the hovercraft at the Northeast Hovercraft Terminal would be *negligible*.	Construction activities for Alternative 2 would have a *moderate* effect on noise, at 72.2 decibels 200 feet away. Road traffic could have an intermittent noise level of 56.5 decibels 50 feet away, which would be a *minor* effect. Noise from the hovercraft would not be present. The overall effect on noise would be *minor*.	Construction and operation activities would have similar *minor* effects as those for Alternative 2.	Alternative 4 has similar effects to that of Alternative 1, and would include 3 additional trips per week and operations year-round. Noise effects do not accumulate over time. Therefore, effects on the noise environment would be expected to remain *negligible*.	Construction activities for Alternative 5 would have a *moderate* effect on noise, at 82.5 dBA from 200 feet away. Operation of the ferry would have an overall *negligible* effect on noise, both because it is quieter than a hovercraft, and hovercraft noise would be eliminated in this alternative. Overall effects of Alternative 5 on noise are considered *negligible*.
Cumulative Effects	Operation of the hovercraft from the Northeast Hovercraft Terminal would result in a *negligible* contribution to cumulative effects on noise.	A project that would have the potential to also affect traffic noise in the area is the completion of the road to the Northeast Hovercraft Terminal. Operations of an additional road would result in a *minor* contribution to cumulative effects on noise.	Cumulative effects associated with Alternative 3 would be similar to cumulative effects associated with Alternative 2. The acreage of the road corridor parcel proposed for exchange would be greater under Alternative 3, but the footprint of the proposed road would be less. The contribution to cumulative effects would be *minor*.	Cumulative effects associated with Alternative 4 would be similar to cumulative effects associated with Alternative 1. Due to the logarithmic nature of additive noise levels, the relative distance to these actions, and the intermittent nature of all of these sources, the cumulative noise effects due to Alternative 4 would be *negligible*.	Noise-generating activities in the area around the ferry operations (boat traffic, aircraft passes, and vehicles, for example) are already included in the background, or ambient noise levels. Alternative 5 would have a *negligible* contribution to cumulative effects on noise.

Terrestrial and Aquatic Plant Communities

	Alternative 1: No Action - Existing Air and Marine Service	Alternative 2: Land Exchange and Southern Road Alignment	Alternative 3: Land Exchange and Central Road Alignment	Alternative 4: Hovercraft Operations from the Northeast Hovercraft Terminal to Cross Wind Cove 6 days per Week	Alternative 5: Lenard Harbor Ferry with Cold Bay Dock Improvement
Overall Effects	There would be *no new effects* on vegetation.	Alternative 2 would result in the addition of approximately 52.583 acres of native cover types (some are non-vegetated) to the National Wildlife Refuge system while relinquishing ownership of 1.820 acres of native cover types; a net gain of approximately 50.763 acres, while also maintaining ownership of 5.430 acres of native cover types on the King Cove Corporation selected parcel. Construction would cause the loss of approximately 107 acres of native plant communities along the proposed road corridor and the loss of less than 1 acre of native vegetation at 2 temporary barge landing sites. The overall effect would be *moderate.*	Alternative 3 would result in the addition of approximately 52.583 acres of native cover types (some are non-vegetated) to the National Wildlife Refuge system while relinquishing ownership of 1.843 acres of native cover types; a net gain of approximately 50.740 acres, while also maintaining ownership of 5.430 acres of native cover types on the King Cove Corporation selected parcel. Construction would engender the loss of approximately 100 acres of native plant communities along the proposed road corridor and the loss of 0.5 acre of native vegetation at 2 temporary barge landing sites. The overall effect would be *moderate.*	Increased operation of the hovercraft from a new location at the Northeast Hovercraft Terminal may create more opportunity for the spread of invasive species in the Izembek National Wildlife Refuge vicinity. The effect would be *minor.*	Invasive species are located in Cold Bay and are also likely present in the King Cove vicinity. These species may be transported to new locations by operation of the ferry terminal. The effect would be *minor.*
Cumulative Effects	There would be *no effects* on vegetation.	Past actions affecting vegetation in or adjacent to the project area are few and minor because this remote location is largely undeveloped. The completion of the road to the Northeast Hovercraft Terminal would contribute to effects on vegetation. The opportunity for invasive species to spread within the Izembek National Wildlife Refuge vicinity would increase. Cumulative effects would be *moderate.*	Cumulative effects would be similar to those discussed under Alternative 2, *moderate.*	The completion of the King Cove Access Project may contribute to effects on vegetation. There would be a *negligible* contribution to cumulative effects to vegetation due to implementation of Alternative 4.	The completion of the King Cove Access Project may contribute to effects on vegetation. There would be a *minor* contribution to cumulative effects to vegetation due to implementation of Alternative 5.

Wetlands

	Alternative 1: No Action - Existing Air and Marine Service	Alternative 2: Land Exchange and Southern Road Alignment	Alternative 3: Land Exchange and Central Road Alignment	Alternative 4: Hovercraft Operations from the Northeast Hovercraft Terminal to Cross Wind Cove 6 days per Week	Alternative 5: Lenard Harbor Ferry with Cold Bay Dock Improvement
Overall Effects	Alternative 1 would result in *no* new effects on wetlands.	Approximately 12.726 acres of wetland would be gained, and 993 relinquished. An estimated total of 3.8 acres of wetland would be filled and 162 drainage structures would be constructed. The effect of modifications to wetland hydrology and vegetation would be *moderate*.	Approximately 12.726 acres of wetland would be gained, and 989 relinquished. An estimated total of 2.4 acres of wetland would be filled and 173 drainage structures would be constructed. The effect of modifications to wetland hydrology and vegetation would be *moderate*.	Effects would be similar to Alternative 1, with *no* new effects identified.	The result of construction of Alternative 5 would include the loss of wetland or wetland functions on less than 1 acre of beach system wetlands. The operation of a ferry would not have any effect on wetlands. The overall impact would be *minor*.
Cumulative Effects	There would be *no effects* on wetlands.	Past actions affecting wetlands in or adjacent to the project area are few and minor because this remote location is largely undeveloped. The completion of the road to the Northeast Hovercraft Terminal would contribute to effects on wetlands. Cumulative effects would be *moderate*.	Effects would be similar to Alternative 2, *moderate*.	Effects would be similar to Alternative 1, with *no* new effects identified.	The completion of the road to the Northeast Hovercraft Terminal involves fill to wetlands. The road from the King Cove Airport to Lenard Harbor also involved fill. Cumulative effects would be *minor*.

Fish and Essential Fish Habitat

	Alternative 1: No Action - Existing Air and Marine Service	Alternative 2: Land Exchange and Southern Road Alignment	Alternative 3: Land Exchange and Central Road Alignment	Alternative 4: Hovercraft Operations from the Northeast Hovercraft Terminal to Cross Wind Cove 6 days per Week	Alternative 5: Lenard Harbor Ferry with Cold Bay Dock Improvement
Overall Effects	There would be no new effects on fish. Continuing noise would have a *negligible* effect on fish.	Alternative 2 involves 8 crossings of anadromous or fish-bearing streams, but effects to anadromous species habitat is not anticipated to be measurable. Increased harvesting pressure on streams could result from increased access. Because of the latter, the effect could be *major*.	Alternative 3 involves 2 crossings of anadromous or fish-bearing streams, but effects to anadromous species habitat is not anticipated to be measurable. Increased harvesting pressure on streams could result from increased access. Because of the latter, the effect could be *major*.	Effects would be similar to Alternative 1, and considered *negligible*.	It is unlikely that essential fish habitat would be affected by dock construction or ferry operation. The effect would be *negligible*.
Cumulative Effects	Effects from the operation and maintenance of Alternative 1 would be primarily associated with vessel noise. There would be a *negligible* contribution to cumulative effects on fish and essential fish habitat under Alternative 1.	Increased harvesting pressure on streams could result from increased access. The cumulative effect, because of established fishing in the area. could be *major*.	Cumulative effects would be similar to those discussed under Alternative 2. *major*.	Effects would be similar to Alternative 1. *negligible*.	Effects would be similar to Alternative 1, and considered *negligible*.

Birds

	Alternative 1: No Action - Existing Air and Marine Service	Alternative 2: Land Exchange and Southern Road Alignment	Alternative 3: Land Exchange and Central Road Alignment	Alternative 4: Hovercraft Operations from the Northeast Hovercraft Terminal to Cross Wind Cove 6 days per Week	Alternative 5: Lenard Harbor Ferry with Cold Bay Dock Improvement
Overall Effects	The use of the hovercraft is most likely to affect seabirds and waterfowl since those groups are more likely to occur in Cold Bay, but it is likely that birds have become habituated to boat and aircraft activities in the area. The overall effect would be *minor*.	The land exchange would result in a net increase in the amount of land managed as national wildlife refuge and wilderness. Izembek Wilderness and its bird habitat would be fragmented by the land exchange. Alternative 2 would have a *major* effect on Tundra Swans, Brant and Emperor Goose, *moderate* effects on other breeding birds and other migrating/wintering birds, and *minor* effects on seabirds.	The land exchange would result in a net increase in the amount of land managed as national wildlife refuge and wilderness. Izembek Wilderness and its bird habitat would be fragmented by the land exchange. Alternative 3 would have a *major* effect on Tundra Swans, Brant and Emperor Goose, *moderate* effects on other breeding birds and other migrating/wintering birds and *minor* effects on seabirds.	The effect of Alternative 4 on birds would be similar to Alternative 1, with slightly higher effects due to the increased frequency of operations. The overall effect would be *minor*.	The noise and sight of the ferry as it crosses the open waters of Cold Bay may startle flocks of seabirds and waterfowl, causing them to alter their behavior. Increased human activity at these locations could cause birds to avoid the areas. Oil or other contaminant leaks from ferry operations are possible and could affect small numbers of seabirds and waterfowl depending on the location and magnitude of the spill, and the prevailing winds. Because the ferry would operate once a day, and the risk of spills is small, the overall effect would be *minor*.
Cumulative Effects	The completion of the King Cove Access Road may result in more waterfowl hunting at Kinzarof Lagoon and the northeast side of Cold Bay, which could disturb other birds as well. The cumulative contribution of Alternative 1 would be *minor*.	Past and present actions that have, and may continue to affect birds in the project area include loss, degradation, and fragmentation of habitat on breeding and wintering grounds and along migratory routes. This includes existing disturbance from local hunters and Cold Bay Airport operations. Alternative 2 would contribute a *moderate* effect on most migratory and breeding birds, *major* for Tundra Swans, Brant and Emperor Goose and a *minor* effect on seabird species.	Cumulative effects would be similar to those discussed under Alternative 2, *minor to major*.	The cumulative effects of Alternative 4 would be similar to that described in Alternative 1, *minor*.	The completion of the King Cove Access Road is expected to result in more human activity and waterfowl hunting at Kinzarof Lagoon and the northeast side of Cold Bay. The overall contribution of Alternative 5 to effects on birds is considered *minor*.

Land Mammals

	Alternative 1: No Action - Existing Air and Marine Service	Alternative 2: Land Exchange and Southern Road Alignment	Alternative 3: Land Exchange and Central Road Alignment	Alternative 4: Hovercraft Operations from the Northeast Hovercraft Terminal to Cross Wind Cove 6 days per Week	Alternative 5: Lenard Harbor Ferry with Cold Bay Dock Improvement
Overall Effects	The noise and sight of the hovercraft as it begins operations at the Northeast Hovercraft Terminal and lands at Cross Wind Cove may startle land mammals, causing them to alter their behavior briefly. The area adjacent to the Northeast Hovercraft Terminal is designated as "medium density – spring, summer, and fall" habitat for brown bear. This site is also designated as "high density – winter range/migration corridor" habitat for caribou, which are considered to be important. Because the frequency of disturbance is low, the summary impact would be *negligible to minor*.	The effect of the land exchange is expected to result in a net increase in the amount of high quality habitat managed in perpetuity for wildlife. Potentially damaging development would not occur because the land would be managed as refuge or wilderness. The acquisition of land in the northern portion of the project area would be beneficial to caribou as it is a high density migration corridor, and it is adjacent to calving areas. Behavior changes, increased human access, and collisions with vehicles could occur with the Alternative 2 road. Effects to brown bears are considered *major* for the isthmus area but *moderate* for the project area. The effects to caribou would also be *moderate*, but the effects could be *major* if caribou migration is interrupted. However, the likelihood of that outcome is judged to be low. The overall effect would be *minor* for small mammals and furbearers and *moderate* for large mammals.	The effects of Alternative 3 are similar to that of Alternative 2. The road's central route could increase potential effects to migrating caribou, and essentially bisects large mammal habitat between Izenbek and Kinzarof lagoons. Effects to brown bears are considered *major* for the isthmus area but *moderate* for the project area. The effects to caribou would also be *moderate*, but the effects could be *major* if caribou migration is interrupted. However, the likelihood of that outcome is judged to be low. The overall effect would be *minor* for small mammals and furbearers and *moderate* for large mammals.	The noise and sight of the hovercraft as it begins operations at the Northeast Hovercraft Terminal and lands at Cross Wind Cove may startle land mammals, causing them to alter their behavior briefly. Because the frequency of disturbance is low, the summary impact would be *minor*.	Although the noise and sight of construction and the operation of the ferry may temporarily startle land mammals, it would be a predictable disturbance occurring in a limited area. Human activities at the Lenard Harbor Ferry Terminal and Cold Bay Dock would likely have a *negligible* effect on land mammals, but the effects on caribou from construction of the terminal could be *minor*.

	Alternative 1: No Action – Existing Air and Marine Service	Alternative 2: Land Exchange and Southern Road Alignment	Alternative 3: Land Exchange and Central Road Alignment	Alternative 4: Hovercraft Operations from the Northeast Hovercraft Terminal to Cross Wind Cove 6 days per Week	Alternative 5: Lenard Harbor Ferry with Cold Bay Dock Improvement
Cumulative Effects	Past and present actions that have, and may continue to, affect land mammals in the project area include sport and subsistence hunting, wildlife trapping, wildlife viewing and management. Because the project area is in a national wildlife refuge, past and present actions that would affect wildlife have been purposefully limited. Very few land-disturbing activities have taken place in the refuge. The completion of the King Cove Access Road (near Izembek National Wildlife Refuge) is expected to result in greater hunter access to large mammals in the project area, and more disturbance in previously undisturbed areas. The overall contribution of Alternative 1 to cumulative effects is considered *negligible*.	Past and present actions that have, and may continue to, affect land mammals in the project area include sport and subsistence hunting, wildlife viewing and management. Because the project area is in a national wildlife refuge, past and present actions that would affect wildlife have been purposefully limited. Very few land-disturbing activities have taken place in the refuge. The completion of the King Cove Access Road (near Izembek National Wildlife Refuge) is expected to result in greater hunter access to large mammals in the project area, and more disturbance in previously undisturbed areas. Alternative 2 would contribute to cumulative effects because of the increase in area readily accessible to humans. The overall effect would be *moderate* to large mammals and *minor* for small mammals and furbearers.	Cumulative effects associated with Alternative 3 would be similar to those associated with Alternative 2. Although potential direct and indirect impacts to caribou could be greater under Alternative 3 because of more proximity to migration patterns, the contribution to cumulative impacts would remain *moderate* to large mammals and *minor* for small mammals and furbearers.	The overall contribution of Alternative 4 to cumulative effects would be considered *minor*, slightly higher than for Alternative 1 because of the increase in weekly frequency and activities during winter use periods by caribou.	The overall contribution of Alternative 5 to cumulative effects would be considered *minor*.

Marine Mammals

	Alternative 1: No Action - Existing Air and Marine Service	Alternative 2: Land Exchange and Southern Road Alignment	Alternative 3: Land Exchange and Central Road Alignment	Alternative 4: Hovercraft Operations from the Northeast Hovercraft Terminal to Cross Wind Cove 6 days per Week	Alternative 5: Lenard Harbor Ferry with Cold Bay Dock Improvement
Overall Effects	Behavioral effects on harbor seals, killer whales, harbor porpoise, and gray whales from the hovercraft operations could occur as a result of vessel noise. However, they are unlikely to leave the area as a result. The no travel zone in the north end of Cold Bay should minimize disturbance effects. The impact of Alternative 1 would be *negligible to minor*.	Construction and operation and maintenance of the southern alignment road is unlikely to affect, killer whales, harbor porpoise, and gray whales. Harbor seals could be slightly affected as they haul out on King Cove Corporation lands adjacent to Kinzarof Lagoon and Sitkinak Island. The summary impact level would be *negligible to minor*.	The effects of Alternative 3 are similar to that of Alternative 2. The summary impact level is considered *negligible to minor*.	Direct and indirect effects of Alternative 4 on harbor seals, killer whales, harbor porpoise, and gray whales, and the mechanisms by which they occur, would be the same as described for Alternative 1. Year-round operation could increase habituation to noise. There would also be seasonal effects, in that some species or their food sources not present in the winter. The overall effect would be *negligible to minor*.	Noise generated from construction activities, including pile-driving, associated with modifications to the existing Cold Bay dock would not likely disturb harbor seals, killer whales, harbor porpoise, and gray whales. Operations would elicit noise similar to fishing vessels already operating in the area, and the ferry would be slow-moving enough that all marine mammals could avert collisions, though they may be temporarily displaced from feeding areas. Effects to marine mammals would be *negligible to minor*.
Cumulative Effects	Past and present actions that have, and may continue to, affect harbor seals, killer whales, harbor porpoise, and gray whales in the project area include commercial fishery-related mortality, entanglement in fishing gear, subsistence harvest and boat strikes. Alternative 1 would result in a *negligible* contribution to cumulative effects.	The contribution to cumulative effects by Alternative 2 is similar to that for Alternative 1, *negligible*.	The contribution to cumulative effects by Alternative 3 is similar to that for Alternative 1, *negligible*.	The contribution to cumulative effects by Alternative 4 is similar to that for Alternative 1, *negligible*.	The contribution to cumulative effects by Alternative 5 is similar to that for Alternative 1, *negligible*.

Threatened and Endangered Species

	Alternative 1: No Action - Existing Air and Marine Service	Alternative 2: Land Exchange and Southern Road Alignment	Alternative 3: Land Exchange and Central Road Alignment	Alternative 4: Hovercraft Operations from the Northeast Hovercraft Terminal to Cross Wind Cove 6 days per Week	Alternative 5: Lenard Harbor Ferry with Cold Bay Dock Improvement
Overall Effects	Given the mitigating restrictions under which the hovercraft previously operated, particularly the exclusion zone in northern Cold Bay, and limited service, disturbance effects on Steller's Eiders, Yellow-billed Loons, Kittlitz's Murrelets, northern sea otters, and Steller sea lions from the operation and maintenance of the hovercraft as proposed under Alternative 1 would be *negligible to minor.*	Construction and operation of the southern road corridor could disturb Steller's Eiders and Yellow-billed Loons during the fall through spring. Eiders are particularly vulnerable to disturbance during pre-migration staging in the spring and the molt in the fall. Kittlitz's Murrelets could be disturbed during the breeding season but the disturbance would be limited to occasional flyovers as they are not expected to nest near the road corridor. Construction and operation of the southern alignment road could elicit disturbance responses from sea otters using northern Kinzarof Lagoon during the summer months. There would be *no effect* to sea lions, as they do not normally occur in the project area. The overall effect to threatened and endangered species would be *minor,* except for Steller's Eiders, which experience *moderate* effects.	The central road alignment could lead to substantial increases in waterfowl hunting pressure in Izembek Lagoon due to improved access for foot and all-terrain vehicles travel. Izembek Lagoon is an important molting area for thousands of Steller's Eiders in the fall, coinciding with the timing of waterfowl hunting for Brant and other species. The direct and indirect impacts are considered *moderate* for Steller's Eiders and *minor* for Yellow-billed Loon, and Kittlitz's Murrelet. Similar to Alternative 2 the effects on sea otters would be *minor,* with *no effects* to Steller sea lions.	The effects of Alternative 4 would be similar to Alternative 1, although the frequency of the hovercraft's operations would increase. Given the mitigating restrictions under which the hovercraft previously operated, particularly the exclusion zone in northern Cold Bay, disturbance effects on Steller's Eiders, Yellow-billed Loons, Kittlitz's Murrelets, Northern Sea Otters, and Steller Sea Lions from the operation and maintenance of the hovercraft as proposed under Alternative 4 would be *negligible to minor.*	Noise generated from construction activities, including pile-driving, associated with modifications to the existing Cold Bay dock would not likely disturb Steller's Eiders, Yellow-billed Loons, or Kittlitz's Murrelets, because they are not present in the summer construction season and/or do not frequent the dock area. Operations would elicit noise similar to fishing vessels already operating in the area, and the ferry would be slow-moving enough that all wildlife could avert collisions. Effects to threatened and endangered species would be *negligible to minor.*

	Alternative 1: No Action - Existing Air and Marine Service	Alternative 2: Land Exchange and Southern Road Alignment	Alternative 3: Land Exchange and Central Road Alignment	Alternative 4: Hovercraft Operations from the Northeast Hovercraft Terminal to Cross Wind Cove 6 days per Week	Alternative 5: Lenard Harbor Ferry with Cold Bay Dock Improvement
Cumulative Effects	The completion of the King Cove Access Road may result in more waterfowl hunting at Kinzarof Lagoon and the northeast side of Cold Bay, which could disturb overwintering Steller's Eiders and Yellow-billed Loons, resting/foraging sea otters and pups, and a few sea lions. The overall contribution to cumulative effects of this alternative would be *negligible* to *minor*.	The contribution of the construction and operation of Alternative 2 to cumulative impacts would include that described in Alternative 1. The overall contribution to cumulative effects of this alternative would be *moderate* for Steller's Eider and *negligible* to *minor* for other threatened and endangered species.	The contribution of the construction and operation of Alternative 3 to cumulative impacts would include that described in Alternative 1. The overall contribution to cumulative effects of this alternative would be *moderate* due to the effects on Steller's Eider.	The contribution of the construction and operation of Alternative 4 to cumulative impacts would include that described in Alternative 1. The overall contribution to cumulative effects of this alternative would be *negligible* to *minor*.	The contribution of the construction and operation of Alternative 5 to cumulative impacts would include that described in Alternative 1. The overall contribution to cumulative effects of this alternative would be *negligible*.

Land Ownership and Use

	Alternative 1: No Action - Existing Air and Marine Service	Alternative 2: Land Exchange and Southern Road Alignment	Alternative 3: Land Exchange and Central Road Alignment	Alternative 4: Hovercraft Operations from the Northeast Hovercraft Terminal to Cross Wind Cove 6 days per Week	Alternative 5: Lenard Harbor Ferry with Cold Bay Dock Improvement
Overall Effects	Under Alternative 1, a road corridor connecting King Cove and Cold Bay would not be built and no land exchange would occur. Current land use would remain unchanged, and management plans would remain in effect. The conveyance of King Cove Corporation selected lands would continue, and includes 5,430 acres currently in Izembek Wilderness. The overall impact of Alternative 1 on land ownership, use, and management would be *minor*.	Under Alternative 2, creation of a road corridor connecting the communities of King Cove and Cold Bay and the associated land exchange involving State, federal and King Cove Corporation lands would have an effect on land use and land management. Federal lands underlying the road corridor and on Sitkinak Island would be transferred to State ownership for management under State Area Plan or State Game Preserve provisions. State owned and King Cove Corporation owned/selected lands would be transferred to or be retained in federal ownership for management under National Wilderness or National Wildlife Refuge provisions. King Cove Corporation would relinquish its selection of the lands east of Kinzarof Lagoon, though they could make a new selection elsewhere. However, the replacement acreage may not have the same characteristics as the selected lands, which directly adjoin patented King Cove Corporation land and are reasonably accessible from the village. The summary impact of Alternative 2 on land use and management would be considered *major*.	The direct and indirect effects on land ownership, use, and management would be nearly identical to Alternative 2. Additional refuge lands would be required for right of way to accommodate this alignment. The summary impact of Alternative 3 on land use and management would be considered *major*.	The effects of Alternative 4, with respect to land ownership, management, and use are identical to those of Alternative 1. The overall impact would be *minor*.	The effects of Alternative 5, with respect to land ownership, management, and use are identical to those of Alternative 1 and 4. The overall impact would be *minor*.

	Alternative 1: No Action - Existing Air and Marine Service	Alternative 2: Land Exchange and Southern Road Alignment	Alternative 3: Land Exchange and Central Road Alignment	Alternative 4: Hovercraft Operations from the Northeast Hovercraft Terminal to Cross Wind Cove 6 days per Week	Alternative 5: Lenard Harbor Ferry with Cold Bay Dock Improvement
Cumulative Effects	Relevant past actions include the entitlement and selection of King Cove Corporation land under ANCSA, and the enactment of ANILCA that designated national wilderness areas throughout the state, including the Izembek Wilderness. The incremental contribution of Alternative 1 to cumulative effects on land ownership, use, and management would be *minor*.	Relevant past actions include the entitlement and selection of King Cove Corporation land under ANCSA, and the enactment of ANILCA that designated national wilderness areas throughout the state, including the Izembek Wilderness. Given the nature and implications of the ownership change, the contribution to cumulative effects would be *major*.	Cumulative effects for Alternative 3 would be nearly identical to Alternative 2, differing only in the location and amount of federal acreage exchanged for the road corridor. The incremental contribution of Alternative 3 to cumulative effects to land use and management would be *major*.	The contribution to cumulative effects for Alternative 4 is the same as Alternative 1 for land ownership, use, and management. The cumulative effect would be *minor*.	The contribution to cumulative effects for Alternative 5 is the same as for Alternatives 1 and 4 for land ownership, use, and management. The cumulative effect would be *minor*.
Socioeconomics					
Overall Effects	While transportation modes and costs are expected to be held constant, the effects to population, demographics and employment would be *negligible*. The Aleutians East Borough would continue to subsidize the hovercraft at roughly $1 million annually, which would be a *moderate* fiscal impact.	Alternative 2 would reduce consumer transportation costs, and eliminate the borough's hovercraft subsidy. There would be few effects to any other socioeconomic indicators. Effects to employment, population and demographics would be *negligible*. Effects to consumer transportation costs and fiscal effects to local governments would be *moderate*.	Alternative 3 would reduce consumer transportation costs, and eliminate the borough's hovercraft subsidy. There would be few effects to any other socioeconomic indicators. Effects to employment, population and demographics would be *negligible*. Effects to consumer transportation costs and fiscal effects to local governments would be *moderate*.	Effects would be similar to Alternative 1. The cost to the consumer would be the same, and effects to population, demographics and employment would be *negligible*. The Aleutians East Borough would continue to subsidize the hovercraft at roughly $2 million annually, which would be a *major* fiscal impact.	Alternative 5 would have *negligible* socioeconomic effects to the cities of King Cove and Cold Bay because the expected changes in employment, economic activity in transportation, and population would be slight. Consumer transportation costs between to the 2 cities would continue in excess of $100 per passenger trip, if vehicle-based travel costs are included. The Aleutians East Borough would subsidize the ferry at more than $2 million annually, which would be a *major* fiscal impact.

	Alternative 1: No Action - Existing Air and Marine Service	Alternative 2: Land Exchange and Southern Road Alignment	Alternative 3: Land Exchange and Central Road Alignment	Alternative 4: Hovercraft Operations from the Northeast Hovercraft Terminal to Cross Wind Cove 6 days per Week	Alternative 5: Lenard Harbor Ferry with Cold Bay Dock Improvement
Cumulative Effects	This alternative would generally perpetuate existing conditions; with *no* additional contributions to cumulative *effects* on socioeconomic indicators.	Fiscal effects to the local government have been previously influenced by a subsidy of the hovercraft operations. This alternative would have a *moderate (beneficial)* contribution to cumulative effects on fiscal resource for local government because of the hovercraft subsidy would cease. Alternative 2 would have a *negligible* contribution to cumulative effects on other socioeconomic indicators.	Fiscal effects to the local government have been previously influenced by a subsidy of the hovercraft operations. This alternative would have a *moderate (beneficial)* contribution to cumulative effects on fiscal resource for local government because of the hovercraft subsidy would cease. Alternative 3 would have a *negligible* contribution to cumulative effects on other socioeconomic indicators.	Fiscal effects to the local government have been previously influenced by a subsidy of the hovercraft operations. This alternative would have a *major (adverse)* contribution to cumulative effects on fiscal resource for local government and a *negligible* contribution to cumulative effects on other socioeconomic indicators.	Fiscal effects to the local government have been previously influenced by a subsidy of the hovercraft operations, and subsidy of a ferry would be possible under Alternative 5. This alternative would have *a major (adverse)* contribution to cumulative effects on fiscal resource for local government and a *negligible* contribution to cumulative effects on other socioeconomic indicators.
Transportation					
Overall Effects	Operation of the hovercraft on a 3-times-a-week schedule provides an additional transportation link for the region, which would benefit approximately 1,000 projected passengers per year. The hovercraft would not operate year-round, and may operate at the previous 70 percent reliability level, reducing opportunity for emergency charters. The summary impact on existing transportation systems and conditions is considered to be *minor*.	A road would add *moderate* traffic to existing transportation facilities over 2 years during the construction phase. Alternative 2 would result in distinctive changes in consumer transportation options, patterns, and costs. The road would provide a new, full-time transportation link between the communities of King Cove and Cold Bay. The summary impact on transportation would be *major*.	The summary effect of Alternative 3 is similar to that of Alternative 2. *major.*	Operation of the hovercraft on a 6-times-a-week, year-round schedule provides an additional transportation link for the region, which would benefit approximately 1,500 projected passengers per year. The former 70 percent reliability level may reduce the opportunity for emergency charters. The summary impact on existing transportation systems, with an increased number of weekly operations, would be *moderate*.	A ferry would provide another form of transportation, besides air, between the cities of King Cove and Cold Bay, benefiting about 1,500 passengers a year. The ferry would operate similarly to that of the prior hovercraft service, with greater frequency and reliability in poor weather. The summary impact for Alternative 5 on transportation is considered to be *moderate*.

	Alternative 1: No Action - Existing Air and Marine Service	Alternative 2: Land Exchange and Southern Road Alignment	Alternative 3: Land Exchange and Central Road Alignment	Alternative 4: Hovercraft Operations from the Northeast Hovercraft Terminal to Cross Wind Cove 6 days per Week	Alternative 5: Lenard Harbor Ferry with Cold Bay Dock Improvement
Cumulative Effects	Public revenues and expenditures have been previously affected by hovercraft operations. Alternative 1 would continue a *moderate (adverse)* fiscal cumulative effect.	The presence of a road could lead to more surface vehicles and increase traffic in both cities over the long-term. Additional traffic could instigate further road improvements and new construction within the communities of King Cove and Cold Bay. The contribution of Alternative 2 to cumulative effects on transportation would be *major.*	The summary cumulative effect of Alternative 3 is similar to that of Alternative 2. *major.*	Public revenues and expenditures have been previously affected by hovercraft operations. Alternative 4 would continue a *major (adverse)* cumulative effect.	Public revenues and expenditures have been previously affected by hovercraft operations. Alternative 5 would continue a *major (adverse)* cumulative effect.

Public Health and Safety

	Alternative 1: No Action - Existing Air and Marine Service	Alternative 2: Land Exchange and Southern Road Alignment	Alternative 3: Land Exchange and Central Road Alignment	Alternative 4: Hovercraft Operations from the Northeast Hovercraft Terminal to Cross Wind Cove 6 days per Week	Alternative 5: Lenard Harbor Ferry with Cold Bay Dock Improvement
Overall Effects	Operation of the hovercraft on a seasonal 3 times a week schedule would not meet community needs for year-round public health and safety. The hovercraft would be available only in the summer months for emergency charters. The summary effect is *minor.*	Under Alternative 2, there would be increased opportunity for people in the City of King Cove to travel to the Cold Bay Airport for access to specialized medical services. Road transportation, while too slow for some emergencies, would be available most days. The road would introduce new law enforcement responsibilities. The summary effect to public health and safety would be *major (beneficial).*	The summary effect of Alternative 3 is similar to that of Alternative 2. *major (beneficial).*	In Alternative 4, the hovercraft would have regularly scheduled trips for 6 days/week year-round and could be available for emergency medical evacuations most times. The historical approximately 70% reliability rate may reduce availability for emergencies, but it could also substitute when weather conditions are adverse for air transport. The summary effect to public health and safety would be *major.*	In Alternative 5, the ferry would have regularly scheduled trips for 6 days/week year-round and would be available for emergency medical evacuations most times. Ferry operations typically have a high reliability rate. It is somewhat slower than other transport options, so may not be suitable for some emergencies. The summary effect to public health and safety would be *major.*
Cumulative Effects	Operation of the hovercraft in Alternative 1 provides a *minor* cumulative effect for public health and safety because there would be an additional option for medical evacuation (hovercraft) for part of the year.	Emergency medical transports have historically been primarily conducted by air and hovercraft. The addition of road transportation, while not suitable for all emergencies, would have a *major* cumulative effect on the range of options available.	The summary cumulative effect of Alternative 3 is similar to that of Alternative 2. *major.*	Operation of the hovercraft in Alternative 4 on a year-round basis provides a *major* contribution to cumulative effects on this resource.	Operation of the ferry in Alternative 5 on a year-round basis provides a *moderate* cumulative effect for public health and safety because it would supplement existing air transport, maximizing opportunity for emergency travel.

Environmental Justice

	Alternative 1: No Action – Existing Air and Marine Service	Alternative 2: Land Exchange and Southern Road Alignment	Alternative 3: Land Exchange and Central Road Alignment	Alternative 4: Hovercraft Operations from the Northeast Hovercraft Terminal to Cross Wind Cove 6 days per Week	Alternative 5: Lenard Harbor Ferry with Cold Bay Dock Improvement
Overall Effects	Alternative 1 would have a *minor (beneficial)* impact on human health and *no new impacts* on subsistence activities. Alternative 1 would not have a disproportionate adverse impact to minority or low income communities. Therefore the summary conclusion is *no adverse effect.*	Alternative 2 would have a *major (beneficial)* impact on human health and a *minor (beneficial)* impact on subsistence activities for the minority and low income communities of King Cove and Cold Bay. Alternative 2 would not have a disproportionate adverse impact to minority or low income communities. Therefore the summary conclusion is *no adverse effect.*	Alternative 3 would have a *major (beneficial)* impact on human health and a *minor (beneficial)* impact on subsistence activities for the minority and low income communities of King Cove and Cold Bay. Alternative 3 would not have a disproportionate adverse impact to minority or low income communities. Therefore the summary conclusion is *no adverse effect.*	Alternative 4 would have a *major (beneficial)* impact on human health and a *negligible (beneficial)* impact on subsistence activities. Alternative 4 would not have a disproportionate adverse impact to minority or low income communities. Therefore the summary conclusion is *no adverse effect.*	In Alternative 5, a ferry would be available year-round to provide transport to Cold Bay under weather conditions not amenable to travel by helicopter, plane, boat, or hovercraft. The direct and indirect effects of ferry operation and maintenance would be a *major* effect for human health and a *negligible (beneficial)* effect to subsistence activities. Alternative 5 would not have a disproportionate adverse impact to minority or low income communities. Therefore the summary conclusion is *no adverse effect.*
Cumulative Effects	The contribution of Alternative 1 to cumulative effects on human health would be *minor*, and would have *no* contribution to cumulative *effects* on subsistence resources and use patterns. Alternative 1 would not have a disproportionate adverse cumulative impact to minority or low income communities.	Alternative 2 would result in *negligible to minor* cumulative effects in access to and competition for subsistence resources. It would result in a *major* cumulative effect in access to health resources, and potential road injuries. Alternative 2 would not have a disproportionate adverse cumulative impact to minority or low income communities.	Alternative 3 would contribute the same cumulative effects as those in Alternative 2. *negligible to minor* for subsistence, and *major* for health. Alternative 3 would not have a disproportionate adverse cumulative impact to minority or low income communities.	Alternative 4 would increase the availability of transportation to medical services as compared to current (baseline) conditions. Implementation of Alternative 4 would not contribute to cumulative effects on subsistence resources, access to subsistence resources, or competition for subsistence resources. Alternative 4 would not have a disproportionate adverse cumulative impact to minority or low income communities.	Alternative 5 would increase the availability of transportation to medical services as compared to current (baseline) conditions. Alternative 5 would not contribute to cumulative effects on subsistence resources. access to subsistence resources, or competition for subsistence resources. Alternative 5 would not have a disproportionate adverse cumulative impact to minority or low income communities.

Public Use

	Alternative 1: No Action - Existing Air and Marine Service	Alternative 2: Land Exchange and Southern Road Alignment	Alternative 3: Land Exchange and Central Road Alignment	Alternative 4: Hovercraft Operations from the Northeast Hovercraft Terminal to Cross Wind Cove 6 days per Week	Alternative 5: Lenard Harbor Ferry with Cold Bay Dock Improvement
Overall Effects	In Alternative 1, there would not be a land exchange and public use of existing parcels would remain the same. The conveyance of a selected parcel to King Cove Corporation would be subject to the requirements of Section 22 (g) of ANCSA. Future public uses of the parcels would be subject to authorization by the private land owner. The overall impact would be *negligible*.	The transfer of state and Native Corporation lands to federal management would restrict activities to those permitted in a wilderness or national wildlife refuge. The exchange would constitute a noticeable change in land management and types of uses. The effects on public use from the land exchange would be *major*.	Alternative 3 would have the same effects as Alternative 2. *major*.	In Alternative 4, there would not be a land exchange and public use of existing parcels would remain the same. The conveyance of a selected parcel to King Cove Corporation would be subject to the requirements of Section 22 (g) of ANCSA. Future public uses of the parcels would be subject to authorization by the private land owner. The overall impact would be *negligible*.	In Alternative 5, there would not be a land exchange and public use of existing parcels would remain the same. The conveyance of a selected parcel to King Cove Corporation would be subject to the requirements of Section 22 (g) of ANCSA. Future public uses of the parcels would be subject to authorization by the private land owner. The overall impact would be *negligible*.
Cumulative Effects	The cumulative impacts of Alternative 1 are considered *negligible*, due to the low levels of use on the parcel selected by the King Cove Corporation.	This alternative could increase opportunities for prohibited access of motorized vehicles. Increased access to hiking areas could expand areas used for berry-picking, photography, and other low-impact public uses. The overall contribution to cumulative effects would be *minor*.	Alternative 3 would have the same contribution to cumulative effects as Alternative 2. *minor*.	The direct and indirect impacts of Alternative 4 are considered *negligible*, due to the low levels of use on the parcel selected by the King Cove Corporation.	The cumulative impacts of Alternative 5 are considered *negligible*, due to the low levels of use on the parcel selected by the King Cove Corporation.

Subsistence

	Alternative 1: No Action - Existing Air and Marine Service	Alternative 2: Land Exchange and Southern Road Alignment	Alternative 3: Land Exchange and Central Road Alignment	Alternative 4: Hovercraft Operations from the Northeast Hovercraft Terminal to Cross Wind Cove 6 days per Week	Alternative 5: Lenard Harbor Ferry with Cold Bay Dock Improvement
Overall Effects	There would be *no new effects* to subsistence under Alternative 1.	Effects from implementation of Alternative 2 could include displacement of subsistence resources increased access to the area around Kinzarof Lagoon. 50,763 acres added to federal subsistence management. and increased competition for resources in that area. The summary impact would be *negligible to minor.*	Alternative 3. the Central Road Alignment, was designed to avoid or minimize impacts to wetlands and high value habitat for breeding. nesting. and migrating waterbirds, and land mammals. As a result, direct effects to these subsistence resources would be lessened. Additionally. 50,737 acres would be added to federal subsistence management. The summary impact would be *negligible to minor.*	Impacts to subsistence would include displacement of subsistence resources. increased access to the area around the Northeast Hovercraft Terminal, and increase subsistence uses in that area. Impacts would be of low intensity. long term in duration, local to regional in extent and affect resources that are common in context. The impact of operation and maintenance activities to subsistence under Alternative 4 would be *negligible.*	The ferry would be operated within concentrated subsistence use areas for waterfowl. salmon. and crab in Lenard Bay. During operation. the ferry would transit through a waterfowl concentration area near Delta Point and Nurse Lagoon on the western side of Cold Bay. Impacts to subsistence would include displacement of subsistence resources. increased access, and increased subsistence uses. The summary impact would be *negligible.*
Cumulative Effects	Alternative 1 would have *no* contribution to cumulative *effects* on subsistence resources or activity.	Alternative 2 would result in *negligible to minor* improvements in access to subsistence resources.	Alternative 3 would result in *negligible to minor* improvements in access to subsistence resources.	Alternative 4 would contribute little to cumulative effects on subsistence resources. access to subsistence resources. or competition for subsistence resource as subsistence activities are unlikely to increase above present levels. The summary cumulative effect would be *negligible.*	Alternative 5 would contribute little to cumulative effects on subsistence resources. access to subsistence resources. or competition for subsistence resource as subsistence activities are unlikely to increase above present levels. The summary cumulative effect would be *negligible.*

Cultural Resources

	Alternative 1: No Action - Existing Air and Southern Marine Service	Alternative 2: Land Exchange and Southern Road Alignment	Alternative 3: Land Exchange and Central Road Alignment	Alternative 4: Hovercraft Operations from the Northeast Hovercraft Terminal to Cross Wind Cove 6 days per Week	Alternative 5: Lenard Harbor Ferry with Cold Bay Dock Improvement
Overall Effects	*No effects* to cultural resources would occur in Alternative 1, since no new actions would occur.	Ground disturbing activities associated with the construction of the road and staging areas could result in direct effects to surface or subsurface prehistoric or historic archaeological sites. Excavation or looting of archaeological sites caused by the introduction of increased access could occur. The summary impact level for cultural resource could be *moderate to major.*	Effects of Alternative 3 are similar to those described under Alternative 2. *moderate to major.*	*No effects* to cultural resources would occur in Alternative 4, since no new actions would occur.	There is low potential for inadvertent damage to previously undetected cultural resources that could occur during the construction or operation of a dock. The summary impact would be *minor.*
Cumulative Effects	*No contribution* to cumulative *effects* to cultural resources would occur in Alternative 1.	Alternative 2 could contribute to cumulative effects on cultural resources. The cumulative effect would be *moderate to major.*	Alternative 3 could contribute to cumulative effects on cultural resources. The cumulative effect would be *moderate to major.*	*No cumulative effects* to cultural resources would occur in Alternative 4.	Cumulative effects to cultural resources for Alternative 5 are considered to be *minor.*

Visual Resources

	Alternative 1: No Action - Existing Air and Marine Service	Alternative 2: Land Exchange and Southern Road Alignment	Alternative 3: Land Exchange and Central Road Alignment	Alternative 4: Hovercraft Operations from the Northeast Hovercraft Terminal to Cross Wind Cove 6 days per Week	Alternative 5: Lenard Harbor Ferry with Cold Bay Dock Improvement
Overall Effects	Air and marine activity would continue at current levels. Such actions are transient, and do not impact vividness, reduce intactness, or reduce unity in existing visual quality. Future use of the King Cove Corporation selected parcel would be subject to the requirements of Section 22 (g) of ANCSA. Overall, the direct and indirect impacts of Alternative 1 are *negligible*.	Alternative 2 would transform the landscape by introducing a road to a currently road less area. The proposed roadway is expected to be compatible with the existing landscape, and the area would retain very high scenic quality. The summary impact would be *moderate*.	Effects of Alternative 3 would be similar to those of Alternative 2. *moderate.* Visual access to the Izembek Lagoon would be improved; however similar benefits would likely not be realized for the Kinzarof Lagoon.	Operation of the hovercraft would introduce weak visual contrast to the surrounding landscape. Movement of the hovercraft across Cold Bay would be noticeable. Periods where the vessel was in view would be episodic and transient. The 6-day operations schedule is expected to be consistent with the landscape character of the communities of King Cove and Cold Bay, and the current use of Cold Bay. Future use of the King Cove Corporation selected parcel would be subject to the requirements of Section 22 (g) of ANCSA. Overall, the direct and indirect impacts of Alternative 4 are *negligible*.	*Minor* effects to visual resources are expected as a result of implementation of Alternative 5. Improvement and use of the Lenard Harbor and Cold Bay docks would contribute in a positive way to the overall landscape character of the communities of King Cove and Cold Bay. The open deck of the ferry would promote access to views of Cold Bay and the surrounding landscape.
Cumulative Effects	Alternative 1 is expected to result in *negligible* cumulative impacts to visual resources.	It is expected that the effects that may result with implementation of Alternative 2 would be additive to those associated with the King Cove Access Road and relocation of the hovercraft terminal. Alternative 2 is expected to have a *moderate* contribution to cumulative effects on visual resources.	It is expected that the effects that may result with implementation of Alternative 3 would be additive to those associated with the King Cove Access Road and relocation of the hovercraft terminal. Alternative 3 is expected to have a *moderate* contribution to cumulative effects on visual resources.	Alternative 4 is expected to result in *negligible* cumulative impacts to visual resources. Consistent use of the hovercraft, combined with the associated roadway and hovercraft terminal would improve the landscape character of the surrounding communities of Cold Bay and King Cove, and would afford additional views of Cold Bay and the surrounding landscape.	The contribution of Alternative 5 is expected to result in overall beneficial impacts to visual resources in the communities of Cold Bay and King Cove. Cumulative effects of the combined actions would be *minor*.

Wilderness

	Alternative 1: No Action - Existing Air and Marine Service	Alternative 2: Land Exchange and Southern Road Alignment	Alternative 3: Land Exchange and Central Road Alignment	Alternative 4: Hovercraft Operations from the Northeast Hovercraft Terminal to Cross Wind Cove 6 days per Week	Alternative 5: Lenard Harbor Ferry with Cold Bay Dock Improvement
Overall Effects	*Minor* impacts to wilderness character would result from noise, and opportunities for use of motorized vehicles off the Northeast Hovercraft Terminal road. The Northeast Hovercraft Terminal road is 0.5 miles from the wilderness boundary.	There would be a total of approximately 131 acres removed from Izembek Wilderness for the road corridor that would follow a southern alignment through the isthmus between Kinzarof Lagoon and Izembek Lagoon. This would fragment approximately 7,665 acres south of the road (excluding Kinzarof Lagoon parcel), interrupting the ecological integrity of the area. An additional 49,921 acres would be added or maintained as wilderness as part of the land exchange. The implementation of Alternative 2 would also result in *major* impacts to the natural quality of wilderness character, *major* impacts to the undeveloped quality, and *major* impacts to the solitude or primitive and unconfined recreation quality. The summary impact on wilderness quality would be *major*.	Effects on Izembek Wilderness resulting from Alternative 3 would be similar to analysis presented under Alternative 2, but with 152 acres removed from the Izembek Wilderness for the road corridor. The location of the Alternative 3 road corridor through the center of the isthmus, as opposed to the more southern alignment of Alternative 2, would create larger sections of fragmented wilderness lands on either side of the corridor. The central road alignment would fragment approximately 11,759 acres of wilderness south of the road corridor (excluding Kinzarof Lagoon parcel) The summary impact on wilderness quality would be *major*.	The increased frequency of hovercraft service to 6 days per week, under Alternative 4 would intensify the localized impacts of hovercraft operations on the opportunity for solitude and the primitive and unconfined recreation quality of the area. Visitors located within the Izembek Wilderness would experience an increase in intermittent noise or visual disturbances in localized areas, through the sights and sounds of vehicles traveling to the Northeast Hovercraft Terminal from the City of King Cove. The summary effect would be *minor to moderate*.	During the construction phase, the operation of heavy equipment, vehicles, and pile driving equipment would produce noise above ambient levels that would be audible from within Izembek Wilderness. Noise disturbances caused by ferry service would not reach the wilderness, and the ferry would be visible from some locations. This would slightly reduce opportunities to experience solitude and primitive recreation within the wilderness. The overall direct and indirect impacts to wilderness character resulting from Alternative 5 would be *minor*.

	Alternative 1: No Action - Existing Air and Marine Service	Alternative 2: Land Exchange and Southern Road Alignment	Alternative 3: Land Exchange and Central Road Alignment	Alternative 4: Hovercraft Operations from the Northeast Hovercraft Terminal to Cross Wind Cove 6 days per Week	Alternative 5: Lenard Harbor Ferry with Cold Bay Dock Improvement
Cumulative Effects	The construction and operation of the King Cove Access Road from Lenard Harbor to the Northeast Hovercraft Terminal would occur from 2011 through late 2012. Portions of the road to the Northeast Hovercraft Terminal would also be visible from localized areas within Izembek Wilderness. Alternative 1 would have a *minor* contribution to cumulative effects on wilderness character within Izembek Wilderness.	The road corridor proposed under Alternative 2 would ultimately connect with the new King Cove Access Road for travel between the cities of King Cove and Cold Bay, and opportunities for unauthorized motorized use in Izembek Wilderness would likely increase beyond current levels. Alternative 2 would have a *major* contribution to cumulative effects on wilderness character within Izembek Wilderness.	The cumulative effects of Alternative 3 would be similar to Alternative 2. *major*.	Cumulative effects to wilderness character within Izembek Wilderness would be *moderate*. The construction of the road to the Northeast Hovercraft Terminal could potentially increase illegal motorized use within Izembek Wilderness on the east side of Cold Bay. The increased frequency of hovercraft operations proposed under Alternative 4 would intensify localized noise disturbance to visitors within Izembek Wilderness.	Alternative 5 would have a *minor* contribution to cumulative effects on wilderness character within Izembek Wilderness.

IZEMBEK NATIONAL WILDLIFE REFUGE
LAND EXCHANGE/ROAD CORRIDOR EIS

U.S. Department of Interior
U.S. Fish & Wildlife Service

http://www.fws.gov
http://izembek.fws.gov/eis.htm

Federal Relay
1 800/877 8339 Voice and TTY

March 2012